ALAN BENNETT has been one of England's
leading dramatists since the success of *Beyond the
Fringe* in the 1960s. His work includes the *Talking
Heads* television series, and the stage plays *Forty
Years On, The Lady in the Van, A Question of Attri-
bution,* and *The Madness of George III,* since made
into a major motion picture. His play *The History
Boys* (also a major motion picture) won six Tony
Awards, including best play, in 2006. His other
books include the critically acclaimed collected
writings *Untold Stories* and *Writing Home, Smut*
(short stories), *The Uncommon Reader* (a novella),
and many more.

Also by Alan Bennett

THE LADY
IN THE VAN

THE LADY
IN THE VAN

And Other Stories

Alan Bennett

PICADOR

New York

picadorusa.com
twitter.com/picadorusa • facebook.com/picadorusa
picadorbookroom.tumblr.com

Picador® is a U.S. registered trademark and is used by St. Martin's Press under license from Pan Books Limited.

For book club information, please visit facebook.com/picadorbookclub or e-mail marketing@picadorusa.com.

"The Lady in the Van" was first published in Great Britain by London Review of Books Ltd., under the title *The Lady in the Van*.

"The Laying On of Hands" was first published in Great Britain by Profile Books, under the title *The Laying On of Hands*.

"Father! Father! Burning Bright" was first published in Great Britain by Profile Books, under the title *Father! Father! Burning Bright*.

Designed by Steven Seighman

Library of Congress Cataloging-in-Publication Data

Bennett, Alan, 1934–
  [Short stories. Selections]
  The lady in the van : and other stories / Alan Bennett.—First edition.
    p. cm.
  ISBN 978-1-250-08972-4 (trade paperback)
  ISBN 978-1-250-08973-1 (e-book)
  I. Title.
  PR6052.E5A6 2015
  823'.914—dc23   2015024391

Our books may be purchased in bulk for promotional, educational, or business use. Please contact your local bookseller or the Macmillan Corporate and Premium Sales Department at 1-800-221-7945, extension 5442, or by e-mail at Macmillan SpecialMarkets@macmillan.com.

First Edition: November 2015

10 9 8 7 6 5 4 3 2 1

Contents

Preface

———✦———

I MOVED TO GLOUCESTER CRESCENT, Camden Town, in 1969. At £11,500, so then hardly a snip, no. 23 was cheaper than some of the other houses because, imposing and double-fronted though it was and built in 1840, it was smaller than most of the villas in the Crescent and so was unsuitable for the young couples with children who were beginning to colonise this part of North London. Built as superior dwellings for the Victorian middle class, the street coincided with the railways that were then being driven through Camden Town (as in *Dombey and Son*) and, partly as a result, the neighbour-hood had gone steadily downhill since, particularly during the Second World War, when many of the villas had been turned into rooming houses. My own house had gas meters in all the upstairs rooms that were a relic of its lodging past and which could still overlap with the present. Early on in my occupancy I opened the door one evening to an old man who was looking for a room there, where he had lodged years ago. At that time I was doing a weekly stint on Ned Sherrin's TV programme *The Late Show* and the old man (played by John Bird) became the central character in a film in which gentrified neighbours with the relics of a social conscience toured Camden Town (in, absurdly, a Rolls-Royce) trying to find other as yet ungentrified lodgings where he would find a welcome. He ended up in the local Rowton House, buildings put up in the nineteenth century to provide respectable working men with bed and board at a reasonable rate.

Though in 1969 there were no longer any lodging houses in the Crescent some council properties survived (which they happily still do), except that given the Thatcherite policy of selling off council tenancies, plus the current financial pressures on local authorities, the status of such properties can hardly be secure. It's a form of social cleansing that has been to the detriment of the street, which is these days more homogenous . . . and homogenously rich . . . than it has ever been.

When I moved in the residents were a mixed bag, with among the earliest to put down roots the artist David Gentleman and his wife, who are still there more than fifty years later. There were journalists like the late Nicholas Tomalin and Claire, his biographer wife, novelists like Nicholas Mosley and Alice Thomas Ellis with her publisher husband, Colin Haycraft, together with Jonathan Miller and his wife, Rachel, who had first seen the For Sale sign go up on no. 23 and alerted me. There was an ex-Yugoslav diplomat, a retired naval commander, the widow of Vaughan Williams, the composer, and round the corner in Regent's Park Terrace the novelist Angus Wilson and his partner, Tony Garrett, who were a few doors along from perhaps the most distinguished denizen of all, the writer and critic V. S. Pritchett. Oh and there was also a bishop, the Anglican Bishop of Edmonton.

What had brought them to this corner of London was that it was unsmart, relatively quiet and handy for Regent's Park and the West End. When I was acting in the theatre I could cycle down to Shaftesbury Avenue in twenty minutes and to the BBC in Portland Place even more quickly. The shopping was good, Inverness Street market just round the corner with a dairy, a bakery and a cobbler's all in the same parade and a nearby assortment of Italian and Asian grocers, a wet fish shop, a couple of bookshops and half a dozen second-hand furniture and junk shops. What there was not was Camden Lock, which in the intervening years has swallowed up the indigenous shops and made the area simply a tourist venue.

Included now are excerpts from my diary for 2014 leading up to the making of the film of *The Lady in the Van* that October, with some interpolations from the introduction to the stage play (1999).

Film Diary

6 January 2014

I've learned never entirely to believe in a film until it actually happens but it does seem likely that this autumn we will be shooting *The Lady in the Van*. This is the story of Miss Mary Shepherd, the elderly eccentric who took up residence in my garden in 1974, living there in a van until her death fifteen years later. Maggie Smith played Miss Shepherd on the stage in 1999 and all being well will star in the film with Nicholas Hytner directing. To date I've written two drafts of the script and am halfway through a third.

The house where the story happened is currently lived in by the photographer Antony Crolla though many of my belongings are still in situ. This afternoon I go round to start the lengthy process of clearing out some of the books and papers so that it can be used for filming.

I first saw the house in 1968. It belonged to an American woman who kept parrots and there were perches in the downstairs room and also in its small garden.

I did most of the decorating myself, picking out the blurred and whitewashed frieze in the drawing room with a nail file, a job that these days would be done by steam cleaning, whereas then I was helped by some of the actors in my first play, *Forty Years On*, which was running in the West End. One of the actors was George Fenton, who is doing the music for the film, and another was Keith McNally, the proprietor of Balthazar.

20 February

The walls of the sitting room and the study in Gloucester Crescent are just as I decorated them nearly half a century ago. I have always been quite proud of my efforts, though aware over the years that the finish I achieved has often been thought eccentric.

In 1969, having stripped the walls down to the plaster, I stained the sitting room blue using a polyurethane stain. The plaster was the original lime plaster put on when the house was built in 1840. Lime plaster has many advantages: it's grainy and doesn't soak up the stain like blotting paper as modern plaster tends to do (and which is often brown or pink). All the blemishes of the lime plaster showed through, including the notes to themselves made by the builders and their occasional graffiti. None of this I minded, but blue was not a good colour; it was too cold and for a while I felt I had ruined the room and would have to paper it, which was the last thing I wanted. Then, as an experiment, I tried some yellow stain on a small patch and this turned the wall a vibrant green, too strong I'm sure for many people but for me ideal, so that's how I did the whole room. The study next door I did differently using water-based stains and as the walls here were lime plaster too I painted them in a mixture of umber and orange, yellow and green. This I then washed down and sealed so that the room ended up far better than I could have imagined, taking on the warm shades of the walls of an Italian palazzo (I thought anyway). I am sure a competent scene painter would have been able to achieve the same effects with much less trouble but I'm happy I did it myself. And in the intervening years the colour has not faded and will I trust continue to glow as long as any new owner suffers the original plaster to remain, which is not long probably as there are few houses on the street left in their original trim, today's newcomers seldom moving in until they have ripped the guts out of these decent Victorian villas to turn them into models of white and modish minimalism.

In the colourful and variegated background of Camden Town Miss Mary Shepherd, whose strange story the film tells, seems in some respects not unusual. She was a vagrant but a stationary one, resident for the last fifteen years of her life a few feet from my front door where there was a paved area . . . the architect had wishfully called it a patio . . . just big enough to take a car. Or, as it transpired, a van.

The neighbourhood has never been without its eccentrics, a steady assortment of which were supplied by Arlington House, one of the Rowton Houses put up in the nineteenth century to provide respectable working men with bed and board at a reasonable rate. And so it admirably did though it also housed some unusual characters, one or two of them straight out of Samuel Beckett. Roaming the streets besides was a cast of itinerant alcoholics who roosted on the steps of any empty premises or the vicinity of any warm-air outlet. If Miss Shepherd stood out in this company it was not as she perhaps imagined on account of some degree of social superiority but because she had, however decrepit, a place of her own in the shape of the van. She never had to sleep in a doorway, for instance, as many of the men did who had not managed to be taken in at Arlington House.

If, at the foot of the slope of Gloucester Crescent, Arlington House was a secular refuge for the poor and homeless, its spiritual counterpart was the convent opposite the top of the street. This unlovely building, now North Bridge House School, was then still a convent which, though I did not know it, had briefly housed Miss Shepherd herself. For much of the time I lived in the Crescent there was a crucifix on its pebble-dashed wall that overlooked the traffic lights of Gloucester Gate and Parkway. Some time in the 1980s the convent was transmuted into a Japanese school, in the process, understandably perhaps, losing the crucifix. Then it became a private school. Though no fan of private education what made me cross was the selfish parking habits of the parents, particularly when retrieving their children. As they park, I used to think, so do they educate.

My decision to invite Miss S. to put the van in my drive in 1974 was taken reluctantly but the construction put upon it in the film seems to me true to the facts. In the street the

van was parked directly opposite the table in the bay window where I did my work. Anything that happened to
Miss Shepherd . . . from the everyday skirmishes she had
with neighbours and passers-by to the more serious provo-
cations regularly visited on her by hooligans or the malevo-
lent . . . all these were a distraction to me when I was trying
to write. Moving Miss S. into the garden got her out of the
way of passers-by and the curious so that both of us could
thereby have a quieter life and I could for much of the time
forget about her—much, as AB points out, like a marriage.

But it was this element of self-interest or self-concern
about the move which has always made me reluctant to consider it an act of charity. I was looking after myself, Miss
Shepherd only incidentally; kindness didn't really come into it.

The idea that marrying is sometimes the way men choose
to forget someone is a (rather crude) Proustian notion, with
Swann wedding Odette in order to do just that. And there
are a cluster of related aphorisms.

'Good nature, or what is often considered as such, is the
most selfish of all the virtues: it is nine times out of ten
mere indolence of disposition.'

This is a quotation from William Hazlitt's 'On the
Knowledge of Character' (1822) but I didn't find it from reading Hazlitt, whom I've never managed to get into, but quoted
in John Osborne's autobiography, *Almost a Gentleman*.

A similar note is struck by George Eliot in *Romola*
(1862–3): 'The elements of kindness and self-indulgence are
hard to distinguish in a soft nature', which is another quotation I did not find at source but quoted in the *Notebooks* of
Geoffrey Madan.

'No man deserves to be praised for his goodness unless he has the strength of character to be wicked. All other goodness is generally nothing but indolence or impotence of will.' (La Rochefoucauld)

The person who never felt the need to go in for such moral analysis and who I'm sure didn't think it was kindness if she ever gave it a thought was, of course, Miss Shepherd herself, parking in my drive a favour she was doing me not the other way round. To have allowed herself to feel in the least bit grateful would have been a chink in her necessary armour, braced as she always was against the world.

'It wasn't a marriage. She wasn't my life,' AB says in one exchange, later cut, though the van always came in handy as a conversation piece. I don't have much small talk so for anyone landed with me at a party, say, 'How's your old lady?' was a good standby. That she had become even in her lifetime something of a celebrity would not have surprised her and she would also consider it entirely fitting that some of her pamphlets are now deposited in the Bodleian Library at Oxford, where Maggie Smith was able to consult them before doing the film.

Miss Shepherd's presence in the garden didn't, of course, stop me jotting things down, making notes on her activities and chronicling her various comic encounters. Indeed, in my bleaker moments it sometimes seemed that this was all there was to note down since nothing else was happening to me.

Still, there was no question of writing or publishing anything about her until she was dead or gone from the garden, and as time passed the two came to seem the same thing. Occasionally newspapers took an interest and tried to blow the situation up into a jolly news item, but the ramparts of privacy were more impregnable in those pre-Murdoch days and she was generally left to herself. Even journalists who came to interview me were often too polite to ask what an (increasingly whiffy) old van was doing parked a few feet from my door. If they did enquire I would explain, while asking them to keep it to themselves, which they invariably did. I can't think that these days there would be similar discretion.

Miss Shepherd helped, lying low if anybody came to my door, and at night straightaway switching off her light whenever she heard a footstep. But though she was undoubtedly a recluse, Miss Shepherd was not averse to the occasional bout of celebrity. I came back one day to find her posing beside the van for a woman columnist (gender did count with Miss S.) who had somehow sweet-talked her into giving an interview, Miss Shepherd managing in the process to imply that I had over the years systematically stifled her voice. If she has since achieved any fame or notoriety through my having written about her, I suspect she would think it no more than her due and that her position as writer of pamphlets and political commentator entitled her to public recognition or, as she says in the play, 'the freedom of the land'.

It was imaginary celebrity—I think the psychological term for it is 'delusion of reference'—that made her assume with every IRA bomb that she was next on the list. A disastrous fire in the Isle of Man meant, she was certain, that the culprit would now target her, and had she been alive at the time of Princess Diana's death she would have taken it as a personal warning to avoid travelling (in the van as distinct from a high-powered Mercedes) under the Pont de l'Alma.

In the first (and much longer) draft of the play this obsession was examined in more detail:

Miss S.: Mr Bennett. Will you look under the van?

AB: What for?

Miss S.: One of these explosive devices. There was another bomb last night and I think I may be the next on the list.

AB: Why you?

Miss S.: Because of Fidelis Party. The IRA may have got wind of it with a view to thwarting of reconciliation attempts, possibly. Look under the van.

AB: I can't see anything because of all your plastic bags.

Miss S.: Yes and the explosive's plastic so it wouldn't show, possibly. Are there any wires? The wireless tells you to look for wires. Nothing that looks like a timing device?

AB: There's an old biscuit tin.

Miss S.: No. That's not a bomb. It's just something that was on offer at Finefare. I ought to have special protection with being a party leader, increased risk through subverting of democracy, possibly.

AB: Nobody knows that you're a leader of a party.

Miss S.: Well, it was on an anonymous footing but somebody may have spilled the beans. No organisation is watertight.

It's said of Robert Lowell that when he regularly went off his head it took the form of thinking he could rub shoulders with Beethoven, Voltaire and other all-time greats, with whom he considered himself to be on equal terms. (Actually, Isaiah Berlin, about whose sanity there was no doubt, made exactly the same assumption but that's by the way.) The Virgin Mary excepted, Miss Shepherd's sights were set rather lower. Her assumed equals were political figures such as former Prime Ministers Harold Wilson, Mr Heath and the Conservative Parliament member Enoch Powell, or as she always called him 'Enoch'. I was constantly being badgered to find out their private addresses so that they could be sent the latest copy of *True View*. Atypically for someone unbalanced, Miss Shepherd never seemed to take much interest in the Royal Family, the Queen and the Duke of Edinburgh never thought of as potential readers.

Miss Shepherd would be no more happy with the notion of AB as her carer than I was . . . and not because 'He's a Communist, possibly'. God apart, she would not presumably have thought herself beholden to anybody . . . hence her seeming ingratitude for any form of benevolence; clothes, vans, crème brulée . . . they all involved obligations for which she had no time. The only obligation that counted was the forgiveness of sin . . . her sin.

We shared, though, a distrust of caring and perhaps the most heartfelt statement I put into the mouth of AB in the film is his diatribe against caring. He does not like the word; is uncomfortable in the role, which it never occurs to him can be so called until it is suggested by the social worker. The word carries an implication of feeling, a coating of concern not just caring but caring *for*, whereas with me, feeling scarcely entered into it and this may well not be uncommon.

Caring, as often as not, is coping with, being landed with, being stuck with, having no choice about. How seldom is it gladly or willingly undertaken? Caring all too often is grudging. Nor is it, as the word implies, a gentle business. 'We have to do everything for her/him means we have to do one thing for them.' Caring is about piss and shit . . . shit on AB's shoes when walking past the van, shit on the path when one of the bags Miss S. hurls out hits the ground and bursts. And these are the most minor inconveniences. I never had to haul down her many contoured underthings to wipe her bum, or haul off her sodden knickers . . . I never had to unfurl her terrible stockings; still less breach the inner citadel of her castle of clothes . . . the routine menialities of real carers, which, we console ourselves, are made tolerable by the love they bear their charges. But one thinks, too, of ageing offspring who are forced into caring for their even more aged parents when all too often they have long since ceased to care for them much or even at all . . . or are only caring for them now in grudging recompense for the caring they themselves received long ago.

With me, kindness was never less kindly nor caring so uncaring with exasperation and self-reproach so often the order of the day.

24 September

I open the paper this morning to find that the Dowager Duchess of Devonshire has died . . . or Debo as everybody

called her, but not me, as when I first got to know her I felt
our acquaintance was too brief for such familiarity and so
ended up calling her 'Ms Debo', while I was 'Mr Alan'. The
darling of the *Spectator* and a stalwart of the Countryside
Alliance, an organisation promoting issues like farming, rural
services and country sports, she was hardly up my street, but
when she wrote asking if I would write an introduction for
one of her books I could not have been more flattered had it
been Virginia Woolf wanting a preface to *Mrs Dalloway*.
Once the request was made, I knew there was no refusing it
and I wrote that the only woman with a will of comparable
iron to Debo was Miss Shepherd. Thereafter Debo signed all
her letters to me 'D. Shepherd', liking the notion that there
might be a seventh Mitford sister, one living in Chatsworth,
the other in a broken-down Commer van.

6 October

The first morning of filming for *The Lady in the Van* and I sit
in what was once my study, the room now bare and cold, the
walls plain plaster, just as it was when I first saw the house in
1968 though I've no memory of being shown it by the estate
agent, which is an early shot in the film. Alex Jennings is playing me and looks remarkably like, with no hint of the outrageous blond there sometimes was in *Cocktail Sticks* when he
played me on the stage.

The cast of *The History Boys* are in the film for sentimen-
tal reasons and because we enjoy working together, even if

some have only one line. Today it's Sam Anderson, now a star of *Doctor Who*, who does the opening shot as a Jehovah's Witness:

'Does Jesus Christ dwell in this house?'

Alex Jennings/AB: 'No. Try the van.'

As always on a film I feel a bit lost, the writer not having a proper function and seldom called upon. After weeks of warm sunny weather today is wet and cold and as Maggie Smith goes out for her first shot she says out of the corner of her mouth, 'Thanks a million.'

7 October

Still not settled in and at one point I find myself perched on top of a dustbin behind the front gate until Sam, the nice PA, finds me a proper seat. I was always led to expect that the director and the stars had their names stencilled on the back of their chosen chairs but in forty or so years filming I've never actually seen it, the productions not grand enough maybe. I know the cameraman Andrew Dunn as he filmed *The Madness of King George* and *The History Boys* and though he's always preoccupied I've never seen him out of temper, so that his benevolence and Nick Hytner's cheerfulness infect the unit. It was not always so, with the cameraman often moodier and more temperamental than the actors. When I started there was almost invariably a degree of ill feeling between the sound department and the camera, with sound complaining that the shot as set up made their job impossible. ('Can't get in there, guv.') That's long gone, the only vestige of it being that sound are generally more forthcoming than the camera crew, who are more self-contained and set more store by their expertise.

Roger Allam and Deborah Findlay play the neighbours opposite, outside whose house Miss Shepherd parks. They aren't modelled on the actual neighbours (who had triplets). The only properly named neighbour is Ursula Vaughan Williams, the composer's widow, who is played by Frances de la Tour. Most of the actors have been in stuff of mine before but not Roger Allam, who has been in practically every play Michael Frayn has written. And I can see why as he's subtle and funny and as good off-screen as on.

Taking it all in is David Gentleman. At eighty-odd he stands for all of two hours together sketching what's going on, delighted at having such a subject on his doorstep.

11 October

Come away around 4.30, weary rather than exhausted as I've contributed very little, my only suggestion being that Alex Jennings, who is eating an egg sandwich, should drop some of the egg down his pullover, as I invariably do. The costume department seize on this as a piece of cinema verité and egg is accordingly smeared down his front. It hardly seems a day's work.

Having two Alan Bennetts was a feature of the stage production though there they were played by different actors. Having them both played by Alex Jennings is harder to establish, particularly at the outset, but the notion that one part of myself dealt with this awkward demanding woman while another part of myself watched myself doing so, often noting it down, was very much what it felt like when it was happening. 'Living,' as Camus said, 'slightly the opposite of expressing'.

There were times, too, when it seemed, grimly affianced as we were, that this was the only thing that was worthy of note, even if Miss Shepherd's presence was so prolonged and taken for granted that the idea I would ever be able to turn it into a book, still less literature, seemed absurd. Also absurd was the notion that she was literary raw material and that this was why I'd invited her in to start with . . . Except of course, if one writes . . . and by the mid 1980s I'd eventually come to the conclusion that this was what I did and that I was indeed 'a writer' . . . then whatever happens is grist to some creative mill, though without any certainty as to its eventual outcome.

15 October

Telling the truth crops up quite a bit in the film, what Miss Shepherd did or didn't do a subject of some disagreement between the two Alan Bennetts. They call not telling the truth 'lying', but 'the imagination' would be a kinder way of putting it, with Alan Bennett the writer finally winning through to make Miss Shepherd talk of her past (as she never actually did) and even to bring her back from the dead in order to take her bodily up to heaven (also imaginary). These departures from the facts were genuinely hard-won and took some coming to, causing me to reflect, not for the first time, that the biggest handicap for a writer is to have had a decent upbringing. Brought up not to lie or show off, I was temperamentally inclined to do both, particularly as a small child, and though reining me in perhaps improved my character it was no help in my future profession, where lying, or romancing anyway, is the essence of it. Nor did my education help. One of the difficulties I had in writing *The Madness of George III* was that, having been educated as a historian, I found it hard ever to take leave of the facts. With George III's first bout of madness the facts needed scarcely any alteration to make them dramatic and only a little tweaking was required but even that I found hard to do.

Never strong on invention I have kept pretty closely to the facts of Miss Shepherd's life, the one exception being the character of the ex-policeman Underwood who figures also in the stage play. He is fictional. That Miss Shepherd had an accident in which a motorcyclist crashed fatally into the van was told me by her brother after her death. It was not her fault but leaving the scene of the accident before the police arrived she was technically guilty of a felony and thus open to blackmail. Underwood is played by Jim Broadbent, with whom I last worked in *The Insurance Man*, a film about Kafka directed by Richard Eyre which we did in Liverpool in 1985, since when Jim has become an international film star much as Pete Postlethwaite did, while seeming no older than he did thirty years back. He's instantly authentic (it's the haircut, I decide), both funny and sinister, and it reminds me how working with him and Julie Walters years ago I used to despair because their casual conversation was funnier and livelier than anything I could dream up. Jim has the ability to look utterly ordinary, certainly in the streets of Camden Town, and though there's no hint of it in the script one would know just from his walk that he's an ex-policeman.

16 October

On one occasion Miss Shepherd claimed to have seen a boa constrictor in Parkway 'and it looked as if it was heading for the van'. At the time I dismissed serpent-sighting as just another of Miss S.'s not infrequent visions . . . boa constrictors, Mr Khrushchev and (putting in regular appearances) the Virgin Mary; the dramatis personae of her visions always rich and varied.

It turned out, however, that on this particular occasion Palmer's, the old-fashioned pet shop in Parkway ('Talking parrots, monkeys, naturalists'), had been broken into, so a boa constrictor on the loose and gliding up the street wasn't entirely out of the question though whether it had a meaningful glint in its eye is more debatable.

This morning we film the sighting of the snake in one of the Gloucester Crescent gardens. And a proper snake it is, too . . . a real boa constrictor, all of nine foot long and answering to the name of Ayesha, which has made the journey from Chipping Norton together with her slightly smaller friend and companion Clementine, both in the care of their handler.

I have had unfortunate experiences with animal handlers as indeed has Maggie Smith, who once had to vault over a stampeding porker during the shooting of *A Private Function*.

To be fair, today's handler seems sensible and (unlike the pig handler) unopinionated and since Ayesha doesn't have anything taxing to do in the way of acting, confines himself to making her and Clementine comfortable on a bed of hot-water bottles.

17 October

We're not shooting in sequence so only ten days into the schedule we do the ending of the film. As written ten years or so after Miss S. died (she died in 1989) I'd imagined a blue plaque to her being unveiled on the wall of no. 23. Nick has made this wittier by having the camera pull back to show today's film crew recording the scene watched by various real-life neighbours from the Crescent. This is also their small reward for their being so forbearing about the inevitable inconvenience the film has involved, except, as I wrote to all of them beforehand, though it would involve them being denied their parking rights for six weeks, housing Miss Shepherd had meant I was deprived of my parking rights for fifteen years. In the event, the scene turns out not quite as I'd imagined. There's a blue plaque on the wall, with a crowd of neighbours including Antony Crolla, who lives in the house, and my (slightly embarrassed) partner Rupert Thomas but then the camera (on a crane) catches me higher up the street as I bike down to the set. I get off my bike and join the crowd as Alex Jennings makes a little speech about Miss S., pulls the cord and the camera dollies back to reveal the rest of the crew. The plaque looks good and genuine, made, I believe out of some rubbery material. I'm hoping it can be left in situ when the film is finished as it may enhance the value of the property thus compensating for the dilapidations consequent on filming and the company getting the house on the cheap.

I have previous form when it comes to unveiling blue plaques as a few years ago I had to pull the cord on the plaque for the peppery painter William Roberts's ex-house in St Mark's Crescent. It's a street that's well supplied with such commemorations. Whereas my own street boasts only one, to Dr Jose Rizal, Writer and National Hero of the Philippines, St Mark's Crescent has at least three, Arthur Hugh Clough, William Roberts and A. J. P. Taylor. There is one to Sylvia Plath where she lived in Chalcot Square but not in Fitzroy Road where she died. The same house, though, has one to Yeats, of whom the late Eric Korn claimed to have heard a passer-by saying, 'Yes, it's a tablet to William Butler Yeast', at which Eric was tempted to add 'who was responsible for the Easter Rising'.

22 October

We are using several vans in varying stages of dilapidation including one smart number in its original trim given to Miss Shepherd some time in the seventies by Lady Wiggin, a Catholic well-wisher from Regent's Park Terrace. Smart as it was, Miss Shepherd still gave it her usual treatment, coating it in lumpy yellow paint (lumpy because she had somehow mixed it with Madeira cake), which she applied with a

washing-up brush. Consequent on these vehicular permutations, for the purposes of filming the contents of one van have
to be taken out and installed in its successor. I sit in my chair
on the pavement watching this wearisome process at work
and marvelling at the dedication and conscientiousness of
Katie Money and the props department who have it to do.
Miss S.'s belongings consist of mountains of old clothes,
carrier bags stuffed with her papers interspersed with the
contents of her larder, half-eaten tins of baked beans,
packets of stale sliced bread, loose onions (which she ate
raw), rotting apples and wilting celery and dressed over all
with half-used toilet rolls, dirty dusters and soiled Kleenex
that one didn't like to look at too closely.

It would be entirely possible to mock up this distasteful
agglomeration with some underlying bean bags, plus a top-
dressing of eye-catching refuse. The camera wouldn't know.
But the actors would. So all this detritus is repeatedly and
meticulously transferred from van to van as if it were the contents of an eighteenth-century salon. I know this devotion
to duty has nothing to do with me personally but I'm the
one who has set it all in motion and I would like to shake all
their hands . . . the boy who carefully transfers the opened
can of congealed tomato soup, Katie who delicately reposi-
tions the dog-eared pack of incontinence pads and puts one of
them to dry, as Miss Shepherd did, over the portable electric
stove top. I am in all their debt. Instead one of them breaks
off to see if she can fetch me a cup of tea.

24 October

Included in the street picture are various passers-by, 'Background action' it's called, as extras walk up or down the street in the back of a scene being played in the foreground. One knows that these characters are actors because they are got up in the fashions of the period and it's particularly noticeable if they're wearing flares or have long hair. The trouble is the street can't be entirely closed off so also coming by are entirely authentic people who are sometimes quite eccentric too and one isn't always sure who are actors and who not. Sometimes, though, it doesn't matter: this morning A. N. Wilson cycles past in his raincoat and beret and he could have been cycling by in 1970.

27 October

Late going round to the unit this morning to find them about to film the scene when manure was being delivered to no. 23, whereupon Miss S. came hurrying over to complain about the stench and to ask me to put a notice up to tell passers-by that the smell was from the manure not her.

Having done one take we are about to go again when it occurs to me that the manure, if fresh, would probably be steaming, as I seem to recall it doing at the time. While this is generally agreed, no one can think of a way of making the (rather straw-orientated) manure we are using steam convincingly. Dry ice won't do it and kettles of hot water prove too laborious. So in the end we go with it unsteaming, the net

result of my intervention being that whereas previously everybody was happy with the shot, now thanks to me it doesn't
seem quite satisfactory.

28 October

We film a scene in which AB is interviewed about his
work by an American journalist, in the course of which he
gives her tea and (though I hadn't specified this) cake.
Props have opted for Battenberg, which is not a confection
I'm much drawn to (I've never liked almond paste), but my
tentative enquiry about the availability of Madeira produces
howls of merriment and so we go with the Battenberg. It's
not that I'm unhappy about this but taken with yesterday's
intervention when I brought the production to a halt over
the steam from the manure I think I must learn to keep my
own counsel.

2 November

Miss S.'s funeral, which in life (or in death) was at Our Lady
of Hal in Arlington Road but in the film is at St Silas's at
the foot of Haverstock Hill. We also film Miss S. at mass
with Maggie Smith at the communion rail. But not just
kneeling. After Miss S.'s death I had a letter from Father
Cormac Rigby, who was twenty years an announcer on BBC
Radio 3 before leaving the Corporation and being ordained
a priest in 1985 when he was sent to live at Our Lady of

Hal, Miss S.'s local church. He told me how seeing her in the congregation his heart would sink as he had a bad back and Miss S.'s exigent (though not ostentatious) piety required her virtually to prostrate herself when receiving the host, with the priest thus having to follow her right down in order to post the wafer in her mouth. Maggie does this, too, on her knees, four or five times without complaint or assistance. She's a few months younger than me but I couldn't kneel like this or if I went down couldn't get up again. She does both and on camera. Now she goes into the confessional box to unburden herself for the umpteenth time to the long-suffering priest (Dermot Crowley), telling him about the motorcyclist she thinks she killed in an accident years ago. He has heard it all before and has absolved her many times. 'Absolution, my child, is not like the bus pass. It does not run out.' Later when the next in the confessional queue (Clive Merrison) enters the box he staggers back on account of the stench she has left behind her. The priest is unsurprised and we hear his tranquil voice, 'There is air freshener behind the crucifix.'

It was Father Cormac Rigby who told me, as much, I felt, out of kindness as conviction, that my taking in Miss Shepherd would speed my passage through Purgatory. I am not banking on it.

6 November

A wet morning and today we are filming Miss S.'s burial in Kensal Green cemetery. In fact she is buried in an unmarked grave in Camden and Islington cemetery out near the North Circular road but Kensal Green is more photogenic. It's cold and drizzling with the actors under umbrellas until the moment before 'Action!' when the puddles are briskly swept from the path before the actors stroll down. At one point I see Andrew Dunn delicately remove a noticeable leaf from the path of the camera with all the care of a caddy setting up a putt in golf. Despite the rain Maggie remains good-tempered if subdued though the moment the shot is called she is straightaway full of energy and in good voice. We look at the dignified grave of Alfred Waterhouse, the Victorian painter, and she becomes hysterical over a family plot with a long list of those here interred which ends up, 'Dora is elsewhere'.

The crucial shot of the day (still raining) comes when the dead Miss Shepherd reappears from the grave and discovers the young biker whom she's always thought she'd killed having a fag behind a gravestone. She walks off with him arm in arm into her own personal sunset and as she does so lets out a cackle. 'Mr Bennett. Do you know what that is? It's the last laugh!' Thereafter . . . and by some technical wizardry I don't understand . . . she will ascend into heaven.

12 November

To the National Theatre where Alex J. is filmed on the stage of the Lyttelton, set up for part of the *Talking Heads* monologue 'A Chip in the Sugar'. It was when we were previewing the stage production at Guildford that I dried three times during the same performance, the stage fright that resulted curing me of any desire to act on the stage. It's a year ago now since the National Theatre Fiftieth Anniversary Gala where I played Richard Griffiths's role in an extract from *The History Boys* and the terror has not subsided. Talk I can do and read but act (and, essentially, remember), not anymore.

13 November

One of the small pleasures of living in Gloucester Crescent/NW1 and one which went unmentioned in the (ever more lavish) brochures put out by the (ever more present) estate agents was waking around six in the morning to the sound of distant horses. Still in those days billeted in St John's Wood the King's Troop regularly exercised in Regent's Park, which would occasionally bring them along Oval Road and down the Crescent. The ancient sound of horsemen carried in the early morning air so one would hear the troop long before they cantered into view, twenty or thirty horses, with each khaki-clad soldier leading another riderless mount.

The mood of this troop was often quite festive and carefree, in spring a rider plucking down a gout of cherry blossom and putting it in his hat, and in winter there would be some sly snowballing. I always got up to watch them go by and on occasion Miss Shepherd would observe her own stand-to, a young soldier once giving her a mock salute. In summer I fancy they were in shirt-sleeve order, but even when they were more formally dressed it was a relaxed performance, which in winter was made more romantic as the riders materialised out of the gloom, preceded by a lone horseman with a lantern, another outrider with a lamp bringing up the rear. Somewhere in London I imagine this spectacle still goes on but St John's Wood Barracks has gone and it's Camden Town's loss—and since the Guards can't trek over from Hyde Park, the film's loss too.

November, Shoreditch Town Hall

Today we film the young Miss Shepherd as the soloist in a symphony concert in the forties playing Chopin's First Piano Concerto.

I lived briefly in Shoreditch when I first came to London in 1961, lodging with some friends from Oxford in Worship Street, cycling to work during the day at the Public Record Office then in Chancery Lane and in the evening at the Fortune Theatre, where I was in the revue *Beyond the Fringe*. The house where we all lived was designed by Philip Webb, the disciple of William Morris, and was something of a social departure, one of a terrace of model dwellings with workshops on the ground floor and accommodation above. Happily it still stands and is now listed. Shoreditch then had little to recommend it, a quarter of small factories and work-shops, greasy spoon cafes and furniture menders. Having scarcely been in the neighbourhood since, I am taken aback by how smart and indeed trendy it seems to be, the Victorian tenements and cottages gentrified, the streets lined with modish shops and eateries. The Town Hall, though, has not changed and its elaborately tiled and plastered hall this morning hosts the London Symphony Orchestra, who are being conducted by George Fenton. Wearing his father's tails he has been given a moustache in order to suggest a young Adrian Boult, the famous conductor . . . a forlorn attempt as Adrian Boult can never have been young and if George looks like anybody it's Flash Harry, Malcolm Sargent. Happily he's not just acting the conductor, having in his time waved his baton (one of Karajan's batons) at the Berlin Philharmonic and the LA Philharmonic. The young soloist, Clare Hammond, plays well too and filmed in longish takes the music is a pleasure to listen to. Half my life is here, I think as I sit listening, as George was in my first play, *Forty Years On*, and learned his music sitting beside the conductor and composer Carl Davis, who played the school organist of Albion House.

I have allowed myself a little leeway in speculating about Miss Shepherd's concert career, except that if, as her brother said, she had studied with Alfred Cortot she must have been a pianist of some ability. Cortot was the leading French pianist between the wars, Miss Shepherd presumably studying with him at the height of his fame. Continuing to give concerts throughout the Occupation, he finished the war under a cloud and it was perhaps this that sent him on a concert tour to England, where I remember seeing his photograph on posters some time in the late forties. Perhaps Miss Shepherd saw it too, though by this time her hopes of a concert career must have been fading, a vocation as a nun already her goal.

Her war had been spent driving ambulances, a job for which she had presumably enlisted and been trained and which marked the beginning of her lifelong fascination with anything on wheels. Comically she figures in my mind alongside the Queen who, as Princess Elizabeth, also did war service and as an ATS recruit was filmed in a famous piece of wartime propaganda changing the wheel on an army lorry, a vehicle my mother fondly believed HRH drove for the duration of hostilities.

What with land girls, nurses, Waafs, the ATS and Wrens, these were years of cheerful, confident, seemingly carefree women and I'd like to think of Miss Shepherd as briefly one of them, having the time of her life: accompanying a singsong in the NAAFI (Navy, Army and Air Force Institutes) perhaps, snatching a meal in a British restaurant, then going to the pictures to see Leslie Howard or Joan Fontaine. It was maybe this taste of wartime independence that later unsuited her for the veil or it may be, as her brother suggested, that she suffered shellshock after a bomb exploded near her ambulance. At any rate she was invalided out and this was when her troubles began, with, in her brother's view, the call of the convent a part of it.

I would have liked her concert career to have outlasted the war or to have resumed after the duration, when the notion of a woman playing the piano against the psychological odds was the theme of the film *The Seventh Veil* (1945) with Ann Todd as the pianist Francesca and James Mason her tyrannical stick-wielding Svengali. Enormously popular at the time (and with it the Grieg Piano Concerto), the film set the tone for a generation of glamorous pianists, best known of whom was Eileen Joyce, who was reputed to change her frock between movements.

The Seventh Veil was subsequently adapted for the stage and I still have the programme of the matinee I saw at the Grand Theatre in Leeds in March 1951. The Grieg Concerto had by this time been replaced by Rachmaninov No. 2 and James Mason by Leo Genn, but it was still Ann Todd, her guardian as ever bringing his stick down across her fingers as she cowered at the keyboard.

If Miss Shepherd had ever made it to the concert circuit this would be when I might have seen her, as I was by now going every week to symphony concerts in Leeds Town Hall where Miss Shepherd would have taken her place alongside Daphne Spottiswoode or Phyllis Sellick, Moura Lympany, Valda Aveling and Gina Bachauer—artistes with their décolleté shawl-collared gowns as glamorous and imposing in my fourteen-year-old eyes as fashion models, Barbara Goalens of the keyboard, brought to their feet by the conductor to acknowledge the applause, clutching to their bosoms the bouquets which they were invariably presented, to which Miss Shepherd on the last night of her life contemptuously compares the scrutty bunch of anemones which AB brings her.

And it was the last night of her life. When I wrote the original account I glossed over the fact that Miss Shepherd's death occurred the same night that, washed and in clean things, she returned from the day centre. I chose not to make this plain because for Miss Shepherd to die then seemed so handy and convenient, just when a writer would (if a little obviously) have chosen for her to die. So I note that I was nervous not only of altering the facts to suit the drama but of even seeming to have altered them.

25 November

Today is the last day of shooting and it's as cold and wet as it was six weeks ago when we started. Today comes the last of the ex-History Boys, Russell Tovey, who plays a dubious youth, and whom I at first don't recognise because of his curly black wig. He only has one line, 'Who's the old bat?' but as he passes the van Maggie has to stick her head out and look after him as he goes.

> Miss S.: Mr Bennett. That young man. Did he have an earring?
> AB: He did.
> Miss S.: You want to be careful . . .

Don't go around saying goodbye as at this stage I'm going to the Wrap Party but when Thursday night comes I can't face it.

There is an odd footnote to Miss Shepherd's story that persists into the present day, as resident in Chiswick until her death quite recently was another lady in a van. This might not seem so odd except that she, too, had been a pianist and was as averse to publicity as Miss Shepherd ever was. When I first heard of her I felt somehow she was a rival and somehow disauthenticated the story of my lady in the van. That's absurd,

xliv | Film Diary

though of one thing I'm sure: Miss Shepherd would not have been pleased.

Miss Shepherd was solipsistic to a degree and, in her persistent refusal to take into account the concerns or feelings of anyone else except herself and her inability to see the world and what happened in it except as it affected her, she behaved more like a man than a woman. I took this undeviating selfishness to have something to do with staying alive. Gratitude, humility, forgiveness or fellow feelings were foreign to her nature or had become so over the years, but had she been otherwise she might not have survived as long as she did. She hated noise, though she made plenty, particularly when sitting in her three-wheeler on a Sunday morning revving the engine to recharge the battery. She hated children. Reluctant to have the police called when the van's window had been broken and herself hurt, she would want the law summoned if there were children playing in the street and making what she considered too much noise or indeed any noise at all.

She inhabited a different world from ordinary humanity, a world in which the Virgin Mary would be encountered outside the Post Office in Parkway and Mr Khrushchev higher up the street; a world in which her advice was welcomed by world leaders and the College of Cardinals took note of her opinion. Seeing herself as the centre of the world, she had great faith in the power of the individual voice, even when it could only be heard through pamphlets photocopied at Prontaprint or read on the pavement outside Williams and Glyn's Bank.

I never questioned Miss Shepherd on the subject but

what intrigued me about the regular appearances put in by the Virgin Mary was that she seldom turned up in her traditional habiliments; no sky-blue veil for her, still less a halo. Before leaving heaven for earth the BVM always seemed to go through the dressing-up box so that she could come down as Queen Victoria, say, or dressed in what sounded very much like a sari. And not only her. One of my father's posthumous appearances was as a Victorian statesman, and an old tramp, grey-haired and not undistinguished, was confidently identified as St Joseph (minus his donkey), just as I was taken briefly for St John.

With their fancy dress and a good deal of gliding about, it was hard not to find Miss Shepherd's visions comic, but they were evidence of a faith that manifestly sustained her and a component of her daily and difficult life. In one of her pamphlets she mentioned the poet Francis Thompson, who was a Catholic as she was (and who lived in similar squalor). Her vision of the intermingling of this world and the next was not unlike his:

> But (when so sad thou canst not sadder)
> Cry:—and upon thy so sore loss
> Shall shine the traffic of Jacob's ladder
> Pitched betwixt heaven and Charing Cross.
>
> Yea, in the night, my Soul, my daughter,
> Cry,—clinging Heaven by the hems;
> And lo, Christ walking on the water
> Not of Gennesareth, but Thames!

It's now over a quarter of a century since Miss Shepherd died, but hearing a van door slide shut will still take me back to the time when she was in the garden. For Marcel, the narrator in Proust's *Remembrance of Things Past*, the sound that took him back was that of the gate of his aunt's idyllic garden; with me it's the door of a broken-down Commer van. The discrepancy is depressing but then most writers discover quite early on that they're not going to be Proust. Besides, I couldn't have heard my own garden gate because in order to deaden the (to her) irritating noise Miss Shepherd had insisted on me putting a piece of chewing gum on the latch.

Alan Bennett, April 2015

The Lady in the Van

Good nature, or what is often considered as such, is the most selfish of all virtues: it is nine times out of ten mere indolence of disposition.

—WILLIAM HAZLITT,
'ON THE KNOWLEDGE OF CHARACTER' (1822)

'I RAN INTO A SNAKE this afternoon,' Miss Shepherd said. 'It was coming up Parkway. It was a long, grey snake—a boa constrictor possibly. It looked poisonous. It was keeping close to the wall and seemed to know its way. I've a feeling it may have been heading for the van.' I was relieved that on this occasion she didn't demand that I ring the police, as she regularly did if anything out of the ordinary occurred. Perhaps this was too out of the ordinary (though it turned out the pet shop in Parkway had been broken into the previous night, so she may have seen a snake). She brought her mug over and I made her a drink, which she took back to the van. 'I thought I'd better tell you,' she said, 'just to be on the safe side. I've had some close shaves with snakes.'

This encounter with the putative boa constrictor was in the summer of 1971, when Miss Shepherd and her van had for some months been at a permanent halt opposite my house

in Camden Town. I had first come across her a few years previously, stood by her van, stalled as usual, near the convent
at the top of the street. The convent (which was to have a
subsequent career as the Japanese School) was a gaunt
reformatory-like building that housed a dwindling garrison
of aged nuns and was notable for a striking crucifix attached
to the wall overlooking the traffic lights. There was something about the position of Christ, pressing himself against
the grim pebbledash beneath the barred windows of the
convent, that called up visions of the Stalag and the search-
light and which had caused us to dub him 'The Christ of
Colditz'. Miss Shepherd, not looking un-crucified herself,
was standing by her vehicle in an attitude with which I was
to become very familiar, left arm extended with the palm flat
against the side of the van indicating ownership, the right
arm summoning anyone who was fool enough to take notice
of her, on this occasion me. Nearly six foot, she was a com-
manding figure, and would have been more so had she not
been kitted out in greasy raincoat, orange skirt, Ben Hogan
golfing-cap and carpet slippers. She would be going on sixty
at this time.

She must have prevailed on me to push the van as far as
Albany Street, though I recall nothing of the exchange. What
I do remember was being overtaken by two policemen in a
panda car as I trundled the van across Gloucester Bridge;
I thought that, as the van was certainly holding up the traffic,
they might have lent a hand. They were wiser than I knew.
The other feature of this first run-in with Miss Shepherd was
her driving technique. Scarcely had I put my shoulder to the
back of the van, an old Bedford, than a long arm was stretched

elegantly out of the driver's window to indicate in textbook fashion that she (or rather I) was moving off. A few yards further on, as we were about to turn into Albany Street, the arm emerged again, twirling elaborately in the air to indicate that we were branching left, the movement done with such boneless grace that this section of the Highway Code might have been choreographed by Petipa with Ulanova at the wheel. Her 'I am coming to a halt' was less poised, as she had plainly not expected me to give up pushing and shouted angrily back that it was the other end of Albany Street she wanted, a mile further on. But I had had enough by this time and left her there, with no thanks for my trouble. Far from it. She even climbed out of the van and came running after me, shouting that I had no business abandoning her, so that passers-by looked at me as if I had done some injury to this pathetic scarecrow. 'Some people!' I suppose I thought, feeling foolish that I'd been taken for a ride (or taken her for one) and cross that I'd fared worse than if I'd never lifted a finger, these mixed feelings to be the invariable aftermath of any transaction involving Miss Shepherd. One seldom was able to do her a good turn without some thoughts of strangulation.

It must have been a year or so after this, and so some time in the late sixties, that the van first appeared in Gloucester Crescent. In those days the street was still a bit of a mixture. Its large semi-detached villas had originally been built to house the Victorian middle class, then it had gone down in the world, and, though it had never entirely decayed, many of the villas degenerated into rooming houses and so were among the earliest candidates for what is now called 'gentrification' but which was then called 'knocking through'. Young professional couples, many of them in journalism or television, bought up the houses, converted them and (an invariable feature of such conversions) knocked the basement rooms together to form a large kitchen/dining-room. In the mid-sixties I wrote a BBC TV series, *Life in NW1*, based on one such family, the Stringalongs, whom Mark Boxer then took over to people a cartoon strip in the *Listener*, and who kept cropping up in his drawings for the rest of his life. What made the social set-up funny was the disparity between the style in which the new arrivals found themselves able to live and their progressive opinions: guilt, put simply, which today's gentrifiers are said famously not to feel (or 'not to have a problem about'). We did have a problem, though I'm not sure we were any better for it. There was a gap between our social position and our social obligations. It was in this gap that Miss Shepherd (in her van) was able to live.

October 1969

When she is not in the van Miss S. spends much of her day sitting on the pavement in Parkway, where she has a pitch outside Williams & Glyn's Bank. She sells tracts, entitled 'True View: Mattering Things', which she writes herself, though this isn't something she will admit. 'I sell them, but so far as the authorship is concerned I'll say they are anonymous and that's as far as I'm prepared to go.' She generally chalks the gist of the current pamphlet on the pavement, though with no attempt at artistry. 'St Francis FLUNG money from him' is today's message, and prospective customers have to step over it to get into the bank. She also makes a few coppers selling pencils. 'A gentleman came the other day and said that the pencil he had bought from me was the best pencil on the market at the present time. It lasted him three months. He'll be back for another one shortly.' D., one of the more conventional neighbours (and not a knocker-through), stops me and says, 'Tell me, is she a *genuine* eccentric?'

April 1970

Today we moved the old lady's van. An obstruction order has been put under the windscreen wiper, stating that it was stationed outside number 63 and is a danger to public health. This order, Miss S. insists, is a statutory order: 'And statutory means standing—in this case standing outside number 63—so, if the van is moved on, the order will be invalid.' Nobody ventures to argue with this, but she can't decide whether her next pitch should be outside number 61 or further on. Eventually she decides there is 'a nice space' outside 62 and plumps for that. My neighbour Nick Tomalin and I heave away at the back of the van, but while she is gracefully indicating that she is moving off (for all of the fifteen feet) the van doesn't budge. 'Have you let the handbrake off?' Nick Tomalin asks. There is a pause. 'I'm just in the process of taking it off.' As we are poised for the move, another Camden Town eccentric materializes, a tall, elderly figure in long overcoat and Homburg hat, with a distinguished grey moustache and in his buttonhole a flag for the Primrose League. He takes off a grubby canary glove and leans a shaking hand against the rear of the van (OLU246), and when we have moved it forward the few statutory feet he puts on his glove again, saying, 'If you should need me I'm just round the corner' (i.e. in Arlington House, the working men's hostel).

I ask Miss S. how long she has had the van. 'Since 1965,' she says, 'though don't spread that around. I got it to put my things in. I came down from St Albans in it, and plan to go back there eventually. I'm just pedalling water at the moment. I've always been in the transport line. Chiefly delivery and chauffeuring. You know,' she says mysteriously—'renovated army vehicles. And I've got good topography. I always have had. I knew Kensington in the blackout.'

This van (there were to be three others in the course of the next twenty years) was originally brown, but by the time it had reached the Crescent it had been given a coat of yellow. Miss S. was fond of yellow ('It's the papal colour') and was never content to leave her vehicles long in their original trim. Sooner or later she could be seen moving slowly round her immobile home, thoughtfully touching up the rust from a tiny tin of primrose paint, looking, in her long dress and sunhat, much as Vanessa Bell would have looked had she gone in for painting Bedford vans. Miss S. never appreciated the difference between car enamel and ordinary gloss paint, and even this she never bothered to mix. The result was that all her vehicles ended up looking as if they had been given a coat of badly made custard or plastered with scrambled egg. Still, there were few occasions on which one saw Miss Shepherd genuinely happy and one of them was when she was putting paint on. A few years before she died she went in for a Reliant Robin (to put more of her things in). It was actually yellow to start with, but that didn't save it from an additional coat, which she applied as Monet might have done, standing back to judge the effect of each brush-stroke. The Reliant stood outside my gate. It was towed away earlier this year, a scatter of yellow drops on the kerb all that remains to mark its final parking place.

January 1971

Charity in Gloucester Crescent takes refined forms. The publishers next door are bringing out some classical volume and to celebrate the event last night held a Roman dinner. This morning the au pair was to be seen knocking at the window of the van with a plate of Roman remains. But Miss S. is never easy to help. After twelve last night I saw her striding up the Crescent waving her stick and telling someone to be off. Then I heard a retreating middle-class voice say plaintively, 'But I only asked if you were all right.'

June 1971

Scarcely a day passes now without some sort of incident involving the old lady. Yesterday evening around ten a sports car swerves over to her side of the road so that the driver, rich, smart and in his twenties, can lean over and bang on the side of the van, presumably to flush out for his grinning girlfriend the old witch who lives there. I shout at him and he sounds his horn and roars off. Miss S. of course wants the police called, but I can't see the point, and indeed around five this morning I wake to find two policemen at much the same game, idly shining their torches in the windows in the hope that she'll wake up and enliven a dull hour of their beat. Tonight a white car reverses dramatically up the street, screeches to a halt beside the van, and a burly young man jumps out and gives the van a terrific shaking. Assuming (hoping, probably) he would have driven off by the time I get outside, I find he's still there, and ask him what the fuck he thinks he's doing. His response is quite mild. 'What's up with you then?' he asks. 'You still on the telly? You nervous? You're trembling all over.' He then calls me a fucking cunt and drives off. After all that, of course, Miss S. isn't in the van at all, so I end up as usual more furious with her than I am with the lout.

These attacks, I'm sure, disturbed my peace of mind more than they did hers. Living in the way she did, every day must have brought such cruelties. Some of the stallholders in the Inverness Street market used to persecute her with medieval relish—and children too, who both inflict and suffer such casual cruelties themselves. One night two drunks systematically smashed all the windows of the van, the flying glass cutting her face. Furious over any small liberty, she was only mildly disturbed by this. 'They may have had too much to drink by mistake,' she said. 'That does occur through not having eaten, possibly. I don't want a case.' She was far more interested in 'a ginger feller I saw in Parkway in company with Mr Khrushchev. Has he disappeared recently?'

But to find such sadism and intolerance so close at hand began actively to depress me, and having to be on the alert for every senseless attack made it impossible to work. There came a day when, after a long succession of such incidents, I suggested that she spend at least the nights in a lean-to at the side of my house. Initially reluctant, as with any change, over the next two years she gradually abandoned the van for the hut.

In giving her sanctuary in my garden and landing myself with a tenancy that went on eventually for fifteen years I was never under any illusion that the impulse was purely charitable. And of course it made me furious that I had been driven to such a pass. But I wanted a quiet life as much as, and possibly more than, she did. In the garden she was at least out of harm's way.

October 1973

I have run a lead out to the lean-to and now regularly have to mend Miss S.'s electric fire, which she keeps fusing by plugging too many appliances into the attachment. I sit on the steps fiddling with the fuse while she squats on her haunches in the hut. 'Aren't you cold? You could come in here. I could light a candle and then it would be a bit warmer. The toad's been in once or twice. He was in here with a slug.

I think he may be in love with the slug. I tried to turn it out and it got very disturbed. I thought he was going to go for me.' She complains that there is not enough room in the shed and suggests I get her a tent, which she could then use to store some of her things. 'It would only be three feet high and by rights ought to be erected in a meadow. Then there are these shatterproof greenhouses. Or something could be done with old raincoats possibly.'

March 1974

The council are introducing parking restrictions in the Crescent. Residents' bays have been provided and yellow lines drawn up the rest of the street. To begin with, the workmen are very understanding, painting the yellow line as far as the van, then beginning again on the other side so that technically it is still legally parked. However, a higher official has now stepped in and served a removal order on it, so all this week there has been a great deal of activity as Miss S. transports cargoes of plastic bags across the road, through the garden and into the hut. While professing faith in divine protection for the van, she is prudently clearing out her belongings against its possible removal. A notice she has written declaring the council's action illegal twirls idly under the windscreen wiper. 'The notice was served on a Sunday. I believe you can serve search warrants on a Sunday but nothing else, possibly. I should have the Freedom of the Land for the good articles I've sold on the economy.' She is particularly concerned about the tyres of the van which 'may be miraculous. They've only been pumped up twice since 1964. If I get another vehicle'—and Lady W. is threatening to buy her one—'I'd like them transferred.'

The old van was towed away in April 1974 and another one provided by Lady W. ('a titled Catholic lady', as Miss S. always referred to her). Happy to run to a new (albeit old) van, Lady W. was understandably not anxious to have it parked outside her front door and eventually, and perhaps by now inevitably, the van and Miss S. ended up in my garden. This van was roadworthy, and Miss S. insisted on being the one to drive it through the gate into the garden, a manoeuvre which once again enabled her to go through her full repertoire of hand signals. Once the van was on site Miss S. applied the handbrake with such determination that, like Excalibur, it could never thereafter be released, rusting so firmly into place that when the van came to be moved ten years later it had to be hoisted over the wall by the council crane.

This van (and its successor, bought in 1983) now occupied a paved area between my front door and the garden gate, the bonnet of the van hard by my front step, its rear door, which Miss S. always used to get in and out of, a few feet from the gate. Callers at the house had to squeeze past the back of the van and come down the side, and while they waited for my door to be opened they would be scrutinized from behind the murky windscreen by Miss Shepherd. If they were unlucky, they would find the rear door open with Miss S. dangling her large white legs over the back. The interior of the van, a midden of old clothes, plastic bags and half-eaten food, was not easy to ignore, but should anyone Miss S. did not know venture to speak to her she would promptly tuck her legs back and wordlessly shut the door. For the first few years of her sojourn in the garden I would try and explain to mystified callers how this situation had arisen, but after a while I ceased to care, and when I didn't mention it nor did anyone else.

At night the impression was haunting. I had run a cable out from the house to give her light and heating, and through the ragged draperies that hung over the windows of the van a visitor would glimpse Miss S.'s spectral figure, often bent over in prayer or lying on her side like an effigy on a tomb, her face resting on one hand, listening to Radio 4. Did she hear any movements she would straightaway switch off the light and wait, like an animal that has been disturbed, until she was sure the coast was clear and could put the light on again. She retired early and would complain if anyone called or left late at night. On one occasion Coral Browne was coming away from the house with her husband, Vincent Price, and they were talking quietly. 'Pipe down,' snapped the voice from the van, 'I'm trying to sleep.' For someone who had brought terror to millions it was an unexpected taste of his own medicine.

December 1974

Miss S. has been explaining to me why the old Bedford (the van not the music-hall) ceased to go, 'possibly'. She had put

in some of her home-made petrol, based on a recipe for petrol substitute she read about several years ago in a news-
paper. 'It was a spoonful of petrol, a gallon of water and a
pinch of something you could get in every High Street.
Well, I got it into my head, I don't know why, that it was
bicarbonate of soda, only I think I was mistaken. It must be
either sodium chloride or sodium nitrate, only I've since been
told sodium chloride is salt and the man in Boots wouldn't sell
me the other, saying it might cause explosions. Though I think
me being an older person he knew I would be more responsible. Though not all old ladies perhaps.'

February 1975

Miss S. rings, and when I open the door she makes a bee-
line for the kitchen stairs. 'I'd like to see you. I've called several times. I wonder whether I can use the toilet first.' I say
I think this is pushing it a bit. 'I'm not pushing it at all. I just
will do the interview better if I can use the toilet first.'
Afterwards she sits down in her green mac and purple
headscarf, the knuckles of one large mottled hand resting on
the clean, scrubbed table and explains how she has devised
a method of 'getting on the wireless'. I was to ask the BBC
to give me a phone-in programme ('something someone like
you could get put on in a jiffy') and then she would ring me
up from the house. 'Either that or I could get on *Petticoat Line*.
I know a darn sight more on moral matters than most of them.
I could sing my song over the telephone. It's a lovely song,
called "The End of the World"' (which is pure *Beyond the*

Fringe). 'I won't commit myself to singing it—not at this moment—but I probably would. Some sense should be said and knowledge known. It could all be anonymous. I could be called The Lady Behind the Curtain. Or A Woman of Britain. You could take a *nom-de-plume* view of it.' This idea of The Woman Behind the Curtain has obviously taken her fancy and she begins to expand on it, demonstrating where the curtain could be, her side of it coincidentally taking in the television and the easy chair. She could be behind the curtain, she explains, do her periodic broadcasts, and the rest of the time 'be a guest at the television and take in some civilization. Perhaps there would be gaps filled with nice classical music. I know one: Prelude and "Liebestraum" by Liszt. I believe he was a Catholic priest. It means "love's dream", only not the sexy stuff. It's the love of God and the sanctification of labour and so on, which would recommend it to celibates like you and me, possibly.' Shocked at this tentative bracketing of our conditions, I quickly get rid of her and, though it's a bitter cold night, open the windows wide to get rid of the smell.

The Woman Behind the Curtain remained a favourite project of hers, and in 1976 she wrote to Aiman (*sic*) Andrews: Now that *This Is Your Life* is ended, having cost too much etc., I might be able to do a bit as The Lady Behind the Curtain. All you need do is put a curtain up to hide me but permit words of sense to come forth in answer to some questions. Sense is needed.' Hygiene was needed too, but possibly in an effort to persuade me about being behind the curtain she brought the subject up herself: 'I'm by nature a very clean person. I have a testimonial for a Clean Room, awarded me some years ago, and my aunt, herself spotless, said I was the cleanest of my mother's children, particularly in the unseen places.' I never fathomed her toilet arrangements. She only once asked me to buy her toilet rolls ('I use them to wipe my face'), but whatever happened in that department I took to be part of some complicated arrangement involving the plastic bags she used to hurl from the van every morning. When she could still manage stairs she did very occasionally use my loo, but I didn't encourage it; it was here, on the threshold of the toilet, that my charity stopped short. Once when I was having some building work done (and was, I suppose, conscious of what the workmen were thinking), I very boldly said there was a smell of urine. 'Well, what can you expect when they're raining bricks down on me all day? And then I think there's a mouse. So that would make a cheesy smell, possibly.'

Miss S.'s daily emergence from the van was highly dramatic. Suddenly and without warning the rear door would be flung open to reveal the tattered draperies that masked the terrible interior. There was a pause, then through the veils would be hurled several bulging plastic sacks. Another pause, before slowly and with great caution one sturdy slippered leg came feeling for the floor before the other followed and one had the first sight of the day's wardrobe. Hats were always a feature: a black railwayman's hat with a long neb worn slightly on the skew so that she looked like a drunken signalman or a French guardsman of the 1880s; there was

her Charlie Brown pitcher's hat; and in June 1977 an oc-
tagonal straw table-mat, tied on with a chiffon scarf and a bit
of cardboard for the peak. She also went in for green eye-
shades. Her skirts had a telescopic appearance, as they had
often been lengthened many times over by the simple expe-
dient of sewing a strip of extra cloth around the hem, though
with no attempt at matching. One skirt was made by sewing several orange dusters together. When she fell foul of
authority she put it down to her clothes. Once, late at night,
the police rang me from Tunbridge Wells. They had picked
her up on the station, thinking her dress was a nightie. She
was indignant. 'Does it look like a nightie? You see lots of
people wearing dresses like this. I don't think this style can
have got to Tunbridge Wells yet.'

Miss S. seldom wore stockings, and alternated between
black pumps and brown carpet slippers. Her hands and feet
were large, and she was what my grandmother would have
called 'a big-boned woman'. She was middle-class and spoke
in a middle-class way, though her querulous and often resent-
ful demeanour tended to obscure this; it wasn't a gentle or
a genteel voice. Running through her vocabulary was a
streak of schoolgirl slang. She wouldn't say she was tired, she
was 'all done up'; petrol was 'juice'; and if she wasn't keen on
doing something she'd say 'I'm darned if I will.' All her conversation was impregnated with the vocabulary of her peculiar brand of Catholic fanaticism ('the dire importance of
justice deeds'). It was the language of the leaflets she wrote,
the 'possibly' with which she ended so many of her sentences
an echo of the 'Subject to the Roman Catholic Church in her
rights etc.' with which she headed every leaflet.

May 1976

I have had some manure delivered for the garden and, since the manure heap is not far from the van, Miss S. is concerned that people passing might think the smell is coming from there. She wants me to put a notice on the gate to the effect that the smell is the manure, not her. I say no, without adding, as I could, that the manure actually smells much nicer.

I am working in the garden when Miss B., the social worker, comes with a boxful of clothes. Miss S. is reluctant to open the van door, as she is listening to *Any Answers*, but eventually she slides on her bottom to the door of the van and examines the clothes. She is unimpressed.

MISS S.: I only asked for one coat.
MISS B.: Well, I brought three just in case you wanted a change.
MISS S.: I haven't got room for three. Besides, I was planning to wash this coat in the near future. That makes four.
MISS B.: This is my old nursing mac.
MISS S.: I have a mac. Besides, green doesn't suit me. Have you got the stick?
MISS B.: No. That's being sent down. It had to be made specially.
MISS S.: Will it be long enough?
MISS B.: Yes. It's a special stick.
MISS S.: I don't want a special stick. I want an ordinary stick. Only longer. Does it have a rubber thing on it?

When Miss B. has gone, Miss S. sits at the door of the van slowly turning over the contents of the box like a chimpanzee, sniffing them and holding them up and muttering to herself.

June 1976

I am sitting on the steps mending my bike when Miss S. emerges for her evening stroll. 'I went to Devon on Saturday,' she said. 'On this frisbee.' I suppose she means freebie, a countrywide concession to pensioners that BR ran last weekend. 'Dawlish I went to. People very nice. The man over the loudspeaker called us Ladies and Gentlemen, and so he should. There was one person shouted, only he wasn't one of us—the son of somebody, I think.' And almost for the first time ever she smiled, and said how they had all been bunched up trying to get into this one carriage, a great crowd, and how she had been hoisted up. 'It would have made a film,' she said. 'I thought of you.' And she stands there in her grimy raincoat, strands of lank grey hair escaping from under her headscarf. I am thankful people had been nice to her, and wonder what the carriage must have been like all that hot afternoon. She then tells me about a programme on Francis Thompson she'd heard on the wireless, how he had tried to become a priest but had felt he had failed in his vocation, and had become a tramp. Then, unusually, she told me a little of her own life, and how she tried to become a nun on two occasions, had undergone instruction as a novice, but was forced to give it up on account of ill-health, and that she had felt for many years that she had failed. But that this was wrong, and it was not a failure. 'If I could have had more modern clothes, longer sleep and better air, possibly, I would have made it.'

'A bit of a spree,' she called her trip to Dawlish. 'My spree.'

June 1977

On this the day of the Jubilee, Miss S. has stuck a paper Union Jack in the cracked back window of the van. It is the only one in the Crescent. Yesterday she was wearing a headscarf and pinned across the front of it a blue Spontex sponge fastened at each side with a large safety pin, the sponge meant to form some kind of peak against the (very watery) sun. It looked like a favour worn by a medieval knight, or a fillet to ward off evil spirits. Still, it was better than last week's effort, an Afrika Korps cap from Lawrence Corner: Miss Shepherd—Desert Fox.

September 1979

Miss S. shows me a photograph she has taken of herself in a cubicle at Waterloo. She is very low in the frame, her mouth pulled down, the photo looking as if it has been taken after death. She is very pleased with it. 'I don't take a good photograph usually. That's the only photograph I've seen looks anything like me.' She wants two copies making of it. I say that it would be easier for her to go back to Waterloo and do two more. No—that would 'take it out of her'. 'I had one taken in France once when I was twenty-one or twenty-two. Had to go into the next village for it. I came out cross-eyed. I saw someone else's photo on their bus-pass and she'd come out looking like a nigger. You don't want to come out like a nigger if you can help it, do you?'

June 1980

Miss S. has gone into her summer rig: a raincoat turned inside out, with brown canvas panels and a large label declaring it the Emerald Weatherproof. This is topped off with a lavender chiffon scarf tied round a sun visor made from an old corn-flakes packet. She asks me to do her some shopping. 'I want a small packet of Eno's, some milk and some jelly babies. The jelly babies aren't urgent. Oh and, Mr Bennett, could you get me one of those little bottles of whisky? I believe Bell's is very good. I don't drink it—I just use it to rub on.'

August 1980

I am filming, and Miss S. sees me leaving early each morning and returning late. Tonight her scrawny hand comes out with a letter marked 'Please consider carefully':

An easier way for Mr Bennett to earn could be possibly with my cooperative part. Two young men could follow me

*in a car, one with a camera to get a funny film like 'Old
Mother Riley Joins Up' possibly. If the car stalls they could
then push it. Or they could go on the buses with her at a
distance. Comedy happens without trying sometimes, or at
least an interesting film covering a Senior Citizen's use of
the buses can occur. One day to Hounslow, another to
Reading or Heathrow. The bus people ought to be pleased,
but it might need their permission. Then Mr Bennett could
put his feet up more and rake it in, possibly.*

October 1980

Miss S. has started hankering after a caravan trailer and has
just missed one she saw in *Exchange and Mart:* 'little net
curtains all round, three bunks'. 'I wouldn't use them all,
except', she says ominously, 'to put things on. Nice little
windows—£275. They said it was sold, only they may have
thought I was just an old tramp . . . I was thinking of offering to help Mrs Thatcher with the economy. I wouldn't ask
any money, as I'm on social security, so it would come cheap
for her. I might ask her for some perks, though. Like a caravan. I would write to her but she's away. I know what's
required. It's perfectly simple: Justice.'

No political party quite catered to Miss S.'s views, though
the National Front came close. She was passionately anti-
Communist, and as long ago as 1945 had written a letter to

Jesus 'concerning the dreadful situation feared from the Yalta agreement'. The trouble was that her political opinions, while never moderate, were always tempered by her idiosyncratic view of the human physiognomy. Older was invariably wiser, which is fair if debatable, except that with Miss S. taller was wiser too. But height had its drawbacks, and it was perhaps because she was tall herself that she believed a person's height added to their burdens, put them under some strain. Hence, though she was in sympathy with Mr Heath on everything except the Common Market, 'I do think that Mr Wilson, personally, may have seen better in regard to Europe, being on the Opposition bench with less salary and being older, smaller and under less strain.' She was vehemently opposed to the Common Market—the 'common' always underlined when she wrote about it on the pavement, as if it were the sheer vulgarity of the economic union she particularly objected to. Never very lucid in her leaflets, she got especially confused over the EEC. 'Not long ago a soul wrote, or else was considering writing [she cannot recall as to which and it may have been something of either] that she disassociated from the Common Market entry and the injustices feared concerning it, or something like that.' 'Enoch', as she invariably called Mr Powell, had got it right, and she wrote him several letters telling him so, but in the absence of a wholly congenial party she founded her own, the Fidelis Party. 'It will be a party caring for Justice (and as such not needing opposition). Justice in the world today with its gigantic ignorant conduct requires the rule of a Good Dictator, possibly.'

Miss S. never regarded herself as being at the bottom of

the social heap. That place was occupied by 'the desperate poor'—i.e. those with no roof over their heads. She herself was 'a cut above those in dire need', and one of her responsibilities in society she saw as interceding for them and for those whose plight she thought Mrs Thatcher had overlooked. Could it be brought to her attention (and she wrote Mrs T. several letters on the subject), alleviation would surely follow.

Occasionally she would write letters to other public figures. In August 1978 it was to the College of Cardinals, then busy electing a Pope. 'Your Eminences. I would like to suggest humbly that an older Pope might be admirable. Height can count towards knowledge too probably.' However this older (and hopefully taller) Pope she was recommending might find the ceremony a bit of a trial, so, ever the expert on headgear, she suggests that 'at the Coronation there could be a not so heavy crown, of light plastic possibly or cardboard for instance.'

February 1981

Miss S. has flu, so I am doing her shopping. I wait every morning by the side window of the van and, with the dark interior and her grimy hand holding back the tattered purple curtain, it is as if I am at the confessional. The chief items this morning are ginger nuts ('very warming') and grape juice. 'I think this is what they must have been drinking at Cana,' she says as I hand her the bottle. 'Jesus wouldn't have

wanted them rolling about drunk, and this is non-alcoholic.
It wouldn't do for everyone, but in my opinion it's better than
champagne.'

October 1981

The curtain is drawn aside this morning and Miss S., still
in what I take to be her nightclothes, talks of 'the discern-
ment of spirits' that enabled her to sense an angelic presence
near her when she was ill. At an earlier period, when she
had her pitch outside the bank, she had sensed a similar
angelic presence, and now, having seen his campaign leaflet,
who should this turn out to be, 'possibly', but Our Conservative Candidate Mr Pasley-Tyler. She embarks on a long
disquisition on her well-worn theme of age in politics. Mrs
Thatcher is too young and travels too much. Not like President Reagan. 'You wouldn't catch him making all those
U-turns round Australia.'

January 1982

'Do you see he's been found, that American soldier?' This is
Colonel Dozo, kidnapped by the Red Brigade and found
after a shoot-out in a flat in Padua. 'Yes, he's been found,'
she says triumphantly, 'and I know who found him.' Thinking it unlikely she has an acquaintance in the Italian version
of the SAS, I ask whom she means. 'St Anthony of course.

The patron saint of lost things. St Anthony of Padua.' 'Well,' I want to say, 'he didn't have far to look.'

May 1982

As I am leaving for Yorkshire, Miss S.'s hand comes out like the Ancient Mariner's: do I know if there are any steps at Leeds Station? 'Why?' I ask warily, thinking she may be having thoughts of camping on my other doorstep. It turns out she just wants somewhere to go for a ride, so I suggest Bristol. 'Yes, I've been to Bristol. On the way back I came through Bath. That looked nice. Some beautifully parked cars.' She then recalls driving her reconditioned army vehicles and taking them up to Derbyshire. 'I did it in the war,' she says. 'Actually I overdid it in the war,' and somehow that is the thin end of the wedge that has landed her up here, yearning for travel on this May morning forty years later.

'Land' is a word Miss S. prefers to 'country'. 'This land . . .' Used in this sense, it's part of the rhetoric if not of madness at any rate of obsession. Jehovah's Witnesses talk of 'this land', and the National Front. Land is country plus destiny— country in the sight of God. Mrs Thatcher talks of 'this land'.

February 1983

A. telephones me in Yorkshire to say that the basement is under three inches of water, the boiler having burst. When told that the basement has been flooded, Miss S.'s only comment is 'What a waste of water.'

April 1983

'I've been having bad nights,' says Miss S., 'but if I were elected I might have better nights.' She wants me to get her nomination papers so that she can stand for Parliament in the coming election. She would be the Fidelis Party candidate. The party, never very numerous, is now considerably reduced. Once she could count on five votes but now there are only two, one of whom is me, and I don't like to tell her I'm in the SDP. Still, I promise to write to the town hall for nomination papers. 'There's no kitty as yet,' she says, 'and I wouldn't want to do any of the meeting people. I'd be no good at that. The secretaries can do that (you get expenses). But I'd be very good at voting—better than they are, probably.'

May 1983

Miss S. asks me to witness her signature on the nomination form. 'I'm signing,' she says: 'are you witnessing?' She has approached various nuns to be her nominees. 'One sister I know would have signed but I haven't seen her for some years and she's got rather confused in the interim. I don't know what I'll do about leaflets. It would have to be an economy job—I couldn't run to the expense. Maybe I'll just write my manifesto on the pavement; that goes round like wildfire.'

May 1983

Miss S. has received her nomination papers. 'What should I describe myself as?' she asks through the window slit. 'I thought Elderly Spinster, possibly. It also says Title. Well my title is'—and she laughs one of her rare laughs—'Mrs Shepherd. That's what some people call me out of politeness. And I don't deny it. Mother Teresa always says she's married to God. I could say I was married to the Good Shepherd, and that's what it's to do with, Parliament, looking after the flock. When I'm elected, do you think I shall have to live in Downing Street or could I run things from the van?'

I speak to her later in the day and the nomination business is beginning to get her down. 'Do you know anything about the Act of 1974? It refers to disqualifications under it. Anyway, it's all giving me a headache. I think there may be another election soon after this one, so it'll have been good preparation anyway.'

June 1984

Miss S. has been looking in *Exchange and Mart* again and has answered an advert for a white Morris Minor. 'It's the kind of car I'm used to—or I used to be used to. I feel the need to be mobile.' I raise the matter of a licence and insurance, which she always treats as tiresome formalities. 'What you don't understand is that I am insured. I am insured in heaven.' She claims that since she had been insured in heaven there has not been a scratch on the van. I point out that this is less to do with the celestial insurance than with the fact that the van is parked the whole time in my garden. She concedes that when she was on the road the van did used to get the occasional knock. 'Somebody came up behind me once and scratched the van. I wanted him to pay something—half-a-crown I think it was. He wouldn't.'

October 1984

Some new staircarpet fitted today. Spotting the old carpet being thrown out, Miss S. says it would be just the thing to put on the roof of the van to deaden the sound of rain. This exchange comes just as I am leaving for work, but I say that I do not want the van festooned with bits of old carpet—it looks bad enough as it is. When I come back in the evening I find half the carpet remnants slung over the roof. I ask Miss S. who has put them there, as she can't have done it herself. 'A friend,' she says mysteriously. 'A well-wisher.' Enraged, I pull down a token piece but the majority of it stays put.

April 1985

Miss S. has written to Mrs Thatcher applying for a post in 'the Ministry of Transport advisory, to do with drink and driving and that'. She also shows me the text of a letter she is proposing to send to the Argentinian Embassy on behalf of General Galtieri. 'What he doesn't understand is that Mrs Thatcher isn't the Iron Lady. It's me.'

To Someone in Charge of Argentina. 19 April 1985

Dear Sir,

I am writing to help mercy towards the poor general who led your forces in the war actually as a person of true knowledge more than might be. I was concerned with Justice, Love and, in a manner of speaking, I was in the war, as it were, shaking hands with your then leader, welcoming him in spirit (it may have been to do with love of Catholic education for Malvinas for instance) greatly meaning kindly negotiators etc. . . . but I fear that he may have thought it was Mrs Thatcher welcoming him in that way and it may hence have unduly influenced him.

Therefore I beg you to have mercy on him indeed. Let him go, reinstate him, if feasible. You may read publicly this letter if you wish to explain mercy etc.

I remain.
  Yours truly
   A Member of the Fidelis Party
    (Servants of Justice)
P.S. Others may have contributed to undue influence also.
P.P.S. Possibly without realizing it.
  Translate into Argentinian if you shd wish.

Sometime in 1980 Miss S. acquired a car, but before she'd managed to have more than a jaunt or two in it ('It's a real goer!') it was stolen and later found stripped and abandoned in the basement of the council flats in Maiden Lane. I went to collect what was left ('though the police may require it for evidence, possibly') and found that even in the short time she'd had the Mini she'd managed to stuff it with the usual quota of plastic bags, kitchen rolls and old blankets, all plentifully doused in talcum powder. When she got a Reliant Robin in 1984 it was much the same, a second wardrobe as much as a second car. Miss Shepherd could afford to splash out on these vehicles because being parked in the garden meant that she had a permanent address, and so qualified for full social security and its various allowances. Since her only outgoings were on food, she was able to put by something and had an account in the Halifax and quite a few savings certificates. Indeed I heard people passing say, 'You know she's a millionaire,' the inference being no one in their right mind would let her live there if she weren't.

Her Reliant saw more action than the Mini, and she would tootle off in it on a Sunday morning, park on Primrose Hill ('The air is better'), and even got as far as Hounslow. More often than not, though, she was happy (and I think she was happy then) just to sit in the Reliant and rev the engine. However, since she generally chose to do this first thing on Sunday morning, it didn't endear her to the neighbours. Besides, what she described as 'a lifetime with motors' had failed to teach her was that revving a car does not charge the battery, so that when it regularly ran down I had to take it out and recharge it, knowing full well this would just mean more revving. ('No,' she insisted, 'I may be going to Cornwall next week, possibly.') This recharging of the battery wasn't really the issue: I was just ashamed to be seen delving under the bonnet of such a joke car.

March 1987

The nuns up the road—or, as Miss S. always refers to them, 'the sisters'—have taken to doing some of her shopping. One of them leaves a bag on the back step of the van this morning. There are the inevitable ginger nuts, and several packets of sanitary towels. I can see these would be difficult articles for her to ask me to get, though to ask a nun to get them would seem quite hard for her too. They form some part of her elaborate toilet arrangements, and are occasionally to be seen laid drying across the soup-encrusted electric ring. As the postman says this morning, 'The smell sometimes knocks you back a bit.'

May 1987

Miss S. wants to spread a blanket over the roof (in addition to the bit of carpet) in order to deaden the sound of the rain. I point out that within a few weeks it will be dank and disgusting. 'No,' she says—'weather-beaten.'

She has put a Conservative poster in the side window of the van. The only person who can see it is me.

This morning she was sitting at the open door of the van and as I edge by she chucks out an empty packet of Ariel. The blanket hanging over the pushchair is covered in washing-powder. 'Have you spilt it?' I inquire. 'No,' she says crossly, irritated at having to explain the obvious. 'That's washing-powder. When it rains, the blanket will get washed.'

As I work at my table now I can see her bending over the pushchair, picking at bits of soap flakes and redistributing them over the blanket. No rain is at the moment forecast.

June 1987

Miss S. has persuaded the social services to allocate her a wheelchair, though what she's really set her heart on is the electric version.

> Miss S.: That boy over the road has one. Why not me?
> Me: He can't walk.
> Miss S: How does he know? He hasn't tried.
> Me: Miss Shepherd, he has spina bifida.
> Miss S: Well, I was round-shouldered as a child. That may not be serious now, but it was quite serious then. I've gone through two wars, an infant in the first and not on full rations, in the ambulances in the second, besides being failed by the ATS. Why should old people be disregarded?

Thwarted in her ambition for a powered chair, Miss S. compensated by acquiring (I never found out where from) a second wheelchair ('in case the other conks out, possibly'). The full inventory of her wheeled vehicles now read: one van; one Reliant Robin; two wheelchairs; one folding pushchair; one folding (two-seater) pushchair. Now and again I would thin out the pushchairs by smuggling one on to a skip. She would put down this disappearance to children (never a favourite), and the number would shortly be made up by yet another wheelie from Reg's junk stall. Miss S. never mastered the technique of self-propulsion in the wheelchair because she refused to use the inner handwheel ('I can't be doing with all that silliness'). Instead, she preferred to punt herself along with two walking-sticks, looking in the process rather like a skier on the flat. Eventually I had to remove the handwheel ('The extra weight affects my health').

July 1987

Miss S. (bright-green visor, purple skirt, brown cardigan, turquoise fluorescent ankle socks) punts her way out through the gate in the wheelchair in a complicated manoeuvre which would be much simplified did she just push the chair out, as well she can. A passer-by takes pity on her, and she is whisked down to the market. Except not quite whisked, because the journey is made more difficult than need be by Miss S.'s refusal to take her feet off the ground, so the Good Samaritan finds himself pushing a wheelchair continually slurred and braked by these large, trailing, carpet-slippered feet. Her legs are so thin now the feet are as slack and flat as those of a camel.

Still, there will be one moment to relish on this, as on all these journeys. When she had been pushed back from the market, she will tell (and it is tell: there is never any thanks) whoever is pushing the chair to leave her opposite the gate but on the crown of the road. Then, when she thinks no one is looking, she lifts her feet, pushes herself off, and freewheels the few yards down to the gate. The look on her face is one of pure pleasure.

October 1987

I have been filming abroad. 'When you were in Yugoslavia,' asks Miss S., 'did you come across the Virgin Mary?' 'No,' I say, 'I don't think so.' 'Oh, well, she's appearing there. She's been appearing there every day for several years.' It's as if I've missed the major tourist attraction.

January 1988

I ask Miss S. if it was her birthday yesterday. She agrees guardedly. 'So you're seventy-seven.' 'Yes. How did you know?' 'I saw it once when you filled out the census form.' I give her a bottle of whisky, explaining that it's just to rub on. 'Oh. Thank you.' Pause. 'Mr Bennett. Don't tell anybody.' 'About the whisky?' 'No. About my birthday.' Pause. 'Mr Bennett.' 'Yes?' 'About the whisky either.'

March 1988

'I've been doing a bit of spring cleaning,' says Miss S., kneeling in front of a Kienholz-like tableau of filth and decay. She says she has been discussing the possibility of a bungalow with the social worker, to which she would be prepared to contribute 'a few hundred or so'. It's possible that the bungalow might be made of asbestos, 'but I could wear a mask. I wouldn't mind that, and of course it would be much better from the fire point of view.' Hands in mittens made from old socks, a sanitary towel drying over the ring, and a glossy leaflet from the Halifax offering 'fabulous investment opportunities'.

April 1988

Miss S. asks me to get Tom M. to take a photograph of her for her new bus-pass. 'That would make a comedy, you know— sitting on a bus and your bus-pass out of date. You could make a fortune out of that with very little work involved, possibly. I was a born tragedian,' she says, 'or a comedian possibly. One or the other anyway. But I didn't realize it at the time. Big feet.' She pushes out her red, unstockinged ankles. 'Big hands.' The fingers stained brown. 'Tall. People trip over me. That's comedy. I wish they didn't, of course. I'd like it easier, but there it is. I'm not suggesting you do it,' she says hastily, feeling perhaps she's come too near self-revelation, 'only it might make people laugh.' All of this is said with a straight face and no hint of a smile, sitting in the wheelchair with her hands pressed between her knees and her baseball cap on.

May 1988

Miss S. sits in her wheelchair in the road, paintpot in hand, dabbing at the bodywork of the Reliant, which she will shortly enter, start, and rev for a contented half-hour before switching off and paddling down the road in her wheelchair. She has been nattering at Tom M. to mend the clutch, but there are conditions. It mustn't be on Sunday, which is the feast of St Peter and St Paul and a day of obligation. Nor can it be the following Sunday apparently, through the Feast of the Assumption falling on the Monday and being transferred back to the previous day. Amid all the chaos of her life and now, I think, more or less incontinent, she trips with fanatical precision through this liturgical minefield.

September 1988

Miss S. has started thinking about a flat again, though not the one the council offered her a few years ago. This time she has her eye on something much closer to home. My home. We had been talking outside, and I left her sitting on the step in the hall while I came back to work. This is often what happens: me sitting at my table, wanting to get on, Miss S. sitting outside rambling. This time she goes on talking about the flat, soliloquizing almost, but knowing that I can hear. 'It need only be a little flat, even a room possibly. Of course, I can't manage stairs, so it would have to be on the ground floor. Though I'd pay to have a lift put in.' (Louder.) 'And the lift wouldn't be wasted. They'd have it for their old age. And they'll have to be thinking about their old age quite soon.' The tone of it is somehow familiar from years ago. Then I realize it's like one of the meant-to-be-overheard soliloquies of Richmal Crompton's William.

Her outfit this morning: orange skirt, made out of three or four large dusters; a striped blue satin jacket; a green headscarf–blue eyeshield topped off by a khaki peaked cap with a skull-and-crossbones badge and Rambo across the peak.

February 1989

Miss S.'s religion is an odd mixture of traditional faith and a belief in the power of positive thinking. This morning, as ever, the Reliant battery is running low and she asks me to fix it. The usual argument takes place:

> ME: Well, of course it's run down. It will run down unless you run the car. Revving up doesn't charge it. The wheels have to go round.
> MISS S.: Stop talking like that. This car is not the same. There are miracles. There is faith. Negative thoughts don't help.

(She presses the starter again and it coughs weakly.) There, you see. The devil's heard you. You shouldn't say negative things.

The interior of the van now indescribable.

March 1989

Miss S. sits in the wheelchair trying to open the sneck of the gate with her walking-stick. She tries it with one end, then reverses the stick and tries with the other. Sitting at my table, trying to work, I watch her idly, much as one would watch an ant trying to get round some obstacle. Now she bangs on the gate to attract the attention of a passer-by. Now she is wailing. Banging and wailing. I go out. She stops wailing, and explains she has her washing to do. As I manoeuvre her through the gate, I ask her if she's fit to go. Yes, only she will need help. I explain that I can't push her there. (Why can't I?) No, she doesn't want that. Would I just push her as far as the corner? I do so. Would I just push her a bit further? I explain that I can't take her to the launderette. (And anyway there is no launderette anymore, so which launderette is she going to?) Eventually, feeling like Fletcher Christian (only not Christian) abandoning Captain Bligh, I leave her in the wheelchair outside Mary H.'s. Someone will come along. I would be more ashamed if I did not feel, even when she is poorly, that she knows exactly what she's about.

March 1989

There is a thin layer of talcum powder around the back door of the van and odd bits of screwed up tissues smeared with what may or may not be shit, though there is no doubt about the main item of litter, which is a stained incontinence pad. My method of retrieving these items would not be unfamiliar at Sellafield. I don rubber gloves, put each hand inside a plastic bag as an additional protection, then, having swept the faecal artefacts together, gingerly pick them up and put them in the bin. 'Those aren't all my rubbish,' comes a voice from the van. 'Some of them blow in under the gate.'

April 1989

Miss S. has asked me to telephone the social services, and I tell her that a social worker will be calling. 'What time?' 'I don't know. But you're not going to be out. You haven't been out for a week.' 'I might be. Miracles do happen. Besides, she may not be able to talk to me. I may not be at the door end of the van. I might be at the other end.' 'So she can talk to you there.' 'And what if I'm in the middle?'

Miss C. thinks her heart is failing. She calls her Mary. I find this strange, though it is of course her name.

April 1989

A staple of Miss S.'s shopping-list these days is sherbet lemons. I have a stock of them in the house, but she insists I invest in yet more so that a perpetual supply of sherbet lemons may never be in doubt. 'I'm on them now. I don't want to have to go off them.'

I ask her if she would like a cup of coffee. 'Well, I wouldn't want you to go to all that trouble. I'll just have half a cup.'

Towards the end of her life Miss S. was befriended by an ex-nurse who lived locally. She put me in touch with a day centre who agreed to take Miss Shepherd in, give her a bath and a medical examination and even a bed in a single room where she could stay if she wanted. In retrospect I see I should have done something on the same lines years before, except that it was only when age and illness had weakened Miss Shepherd that she would accept such help. Even then it was not easy.

27 April 1989

A red ambulance calls to take Miss S. to the day centre. Miss B. talks to her for a while in the van, gradually coaxing her out and into the wheelchair, shit streaks over her swollen feet, a piece of toilet roll clinging to one scaly ankle. 'And if I don't like it,' she keeps asking, 'can I come back?' I reassure her, but, looking at the inside of the van and trying to cope with the stench, I find it hard to see how she can go on living here much longer. Once she sees the room they are offering her, the bath, the clean sheets, I can't imagine her wanting to come back. And indeed she makes more fuss than usual about locking the van door, which suggests she accepts that she may not be returning. I note how, with none of my distaste, the ambulance driver bends over her as he puts her on the hoist, his careful rearrangement of her greasy clothing, pulling her skirt down over her knees in the interests of modesty. The chair goes on the hoist, and slowly she rises and comes into view above the level of the garden wall and is wheeled into the ambulance. There is a certain distinction about her as she leaves, a Dorothy Hodgkin of vagabonds, a derelict Nobel Prize winner, the heavy folds of her grimy face set in a kind of resigned satisfaction. She may even be enjoying herself.

When she has gone I walk round the van noting the occasions of our battle: the carpet tiles she managed to smuggle on to the roof, the blanket strapped on to muffle the sound of the rain, the black bags under the van stuffed with her old clothes—sites of skirmishes all of which I'd lost. Now I imagine her bathed and bandaged and cleanly clothed and starting a new life. I even see myself visiting and taking flowers.

This fantasy rapidly fades when around 2.30 Miss S. reappears, washed and in clean clothes, it's true, and with a long pair of white hospital socks over her shrunken legs, but obviously very pleased to be back. She has a telephone number where her new friends can be contacted, and she gives it to me. 'They can be reached', she says, 'any time—even over the holiday. They're on a long-distance bleep.'

As I am leaving for the theatre, she bangs on the door of the van with her stick. I open the door. She is lying wrapped in clean white sheets on a quilt laid over all the accumulated filth and rubbish of the van. She is still worrying that I will have her taken to hospital. I tell her there's no question of it and that she can stay as long as she wants. I close the door, but there is another bang and I reassure her again. Once more I close the door, but she bangs again. 'Mr Bennett.' I have to strain to hear. 'I'm sorry the van's in such a state. I haven't been able to do any spring cleaning.'

28 April

I am working at my table when I see Miss B. arrive with a pile of clean clothes for Miss Shepherd, which must have been washed for her at the day centre yesterday. Miss B. knocks at the door of the van, then opens it, looks inside and—something nobody has ever done before—gets in. It's only a moment before she comes out, and I know what has happened before she rings the bell. We go back to the van where Miss Shepherd is dead, lying on her left side, flesh cold, face gaunt, the neck stretched out as if for the block, and a bee buzzing round her body.

It is a beautiful day, with the garden glittering in the sunshine, strong shadows by the nettles, and bluebells out under the wall, and I remember how in her occasional moments of contemplation she would sit in the wheelchair and gaze at the garden. I am filled with remorse for my harsh conduct towards her, though I know at the same time that it was not harsh. But still I never quite believed or chose to believe she was as ill as she was, and I regret too all the questions I never asked her. Not that she would have answered them. I have a strong impulse to stand at the gate and tell anyone who passes.

Miss B. meanwhile goes off and returns with a nice doctor from St Pancras who seems scarcely out of her teens. She gets into the van, takes the pulse in Miss S.'s outstretched neck, checks her with a stethoscope and, to save an autopsy, certifies death as from heart failure. Then comes the priest to bless her before she is taken to the funeral parlour, and he, too, gets into the van—the third person to do so this morning, and all of them without distaste or ado in what to me seem three small acts of heroism. Stooping over the body, his bright white hair brushing the top of the van, the priest murmurs an inaudible prayer and makes a cross on Miss S.'s hands and head. Then they all go off and I come inside to wait for the undertakers.

I have been sitting at my table for ten minutes before I realize that the undertakers have been here all the time, and that death nowadays comes (or goes) in a grey Ford transit van that is standing outside the gate. There are three undertakers, two young and burly, the third older and more experienced—a sergeant, as it were, and two corporals. They bring out a rough grey-painted coffin, like a prop a conjuror might use, and, making no comment on the surely extraordinary circumstances in which they find it, put a sheet of white plastic bin-liner over the body and manhandle it into their magic box, where it falls with a bit of a thud. Across the road, office workers stroll down from the Piano Factory for their lunch, but nobody stops or even looks much, and the Asian woman who has to wait while the box is carried over the pavement and put in the (other) van doesn't give it a backward glance.

Later I go round to the undertakers to arrange the funeral, and the manager apologizes for their response when I had originally phoned. A woman had answered, saying, 'What exactly is it you want?' Not thinking callers rang undertakers with a great variety of requests, I was nonplussed. Then she said briskly, 'Do you want someone taking away?' The undertaker explains that her seemingly unhelpful manner was because she thought my call wasn't genuine. 'We get so many hoaxes these days. I've often gone round to collect a corpse only to have it open the door.'

9 May

Miss Shepherd's funeral is at Our Lady of Hal, the Catholic church round the corner. The service has been slotted into the ten o'clock mass, so that, in addition to a contingent of neighbours, the congregation includes what I take to be regulars: the fat little man in thick glasses and trainers who hobbles along to the church every day from Arlington House; several nuns, among them the ninety-nine-year-old sister who was in charge when Miss S. was briefly a novice; a woman in a green straw hat like an upturned plant pot who eats toffees throughout; and another lady who plays the harmonium in tan slacks and a tea-cosy wig. The server, a middle-aged man with white hair, doesn't wear a surplice, just ordinary clothes with an open-necked shirt, and, but for knowing all the sacred drill, might have been roped in from the group on the corner outside The Good Mixer. The priest is a young Irish boy with a big, red peasant face and sandy hair, and he, too, stripped of his cream-coloured cassock, could be wielding a pneumatic drill in the roadworks outside. I keep thinking about these characters during the terrible service, and it re-inforces what I have always known: that I could never be a Catholic because I'm such a snob, and that the biggest sacri-fice Newman made when he turned his back on the C of E was the social one.

Yet kindness abounds. In front of us is a thin old man who

knows the service backwards, and seeing we have no prayer books he lays down his own on top of his copy of the *Sun*, goes back up the aisle to fetch us some, and hands them round, all the time saying the responses without faltering. The first hymn is Newman's 'Lead Kindly Light', which I try and sing, while making no attempt at the second hymn, which is 'Kum Ba Ya'. The priest turns out to have a good strong voice, though its tone is more suited to 'Kum Ba Ya' than to Newman and J. B. Dykes. The service itself is wet and wandering, even more so than the current Anglican equivalent, though occasionally one catches in the watered-down language a distant echo of 1662. Now, though, arrives the bit I dread, the celebration of fellowship, which always reminds me of the warm-up Ned Sherrin insisted on inflicting on the studio audience before *Not So Much a Programme*, when everyone had to shake hands with their neighbour. But again the nice man who fetched us the prayer books shames me when he turns round without any fuss or embarrassment and smilingly shakes my hand. Then it is the mass proper, the priest distributing the wafers to the ninety-nine-year-old nun and the lady with the plant pot on her head, as Miss S. lies in her coffin at his elbow. Finally there is another hymn, this one by the (to me) unknown hymnodist Kevin Norton, who's obviously reworked it from his unsuccessful entry for the Eurovision Song Contest; and with the young priest acting as lead singer, and the congregation a rather subdued backing group, Miss Shepherd is carried out.

The neighbours, who are not quite mourners, wait on the pavement outside as the coffin is hoisted on to the hearse. 'A cut above her previous vehicle,' remarks Colin H.; and comedy persists when the car accompanying the hearse to the cemetery refuses to start. It's a familiar scene, and one which I've played many times, with Miss S. waiting inside her vehicle as well-wishers lift the bonnet, fetch leads and give it a jump start. Except this time she's dead.

Only A. and I and Clare, the ex-nurse who lately befriended Miss S., accompany the body, swept around Hampstead Heath at a less than funereal pace, down Bishop's Avenue and up to the St Pancras Cemetery, green and lush this warm, sunny day. We drive beyond the scattered woods to the furthest edge where stand long lines of new gravestones, mostly in black polished granite. Appropriately, in view of her lifelong love of the car, Miss S. is being buried within sight and sound of the North Circular Road, one carriageway the other side of the hedge, with juggernauts drowning the words of the priest as he commits the body to the earth. He gives us each a go with his little plastic bottle of holy water, we throw some soil into the grave, and then everybody leaves me to whatever solitary thoughts I might have, which are not many, before we are driven back to Camden Town—life reasserted when the undertaker drops us handily outside Sainsbury's.

In the interval between Miss Shepherd's death and her funeral ten days later I found out more about her life than I had in twenty years. She had indeed driven ambulances during the war, and was either blown up or narrowly escaped death when a bomb exploded nearby. I'm not sure that her eccentricity can be put down to this any more than to the legend, mentioned by one of the nuns, that it was the death of her fiancé in this incident that 'tipped her over'. It would be comforting to think that it is love, or the death of it, that un-balances the mind, but I think her early attempts to become a nun and her repeated failures ('too argumentative,' one of the sisters said) point to a personality that must already have been quite awkward when she was a girl. After the war she spent some time in mental hospitals, but regularly absconded, fi-nally remaining at large long enough to establish her com-petence to live unsupervised.

The turning-point in her life came when, through no fault of hers, a motorcyclist crashed into the side of her van. If her other vans were any guide, this one too would only have been insured in heaven, so it's not surprising she left the scene of the accident ('skedaddled', she would have said) without giving her name or address. The motorcyclist subsequently died, so that, while blameless in the accident, by leaving the scene of it she had committed a criminal offence. The police mounted a search for her. Having already changed her first name when she became a novice, now under very different circumstances she changed her second and, calling herself Shepherd, made her way back to Camden Town and the vi-cinity of the convent where she had taken her vows. And though in the years to come she had little to do with the nuns, or they with her, she was never to stray far from the convent for the rest of her life.

All this I learned in those last few days. It was as if she had been a character in Dickens whose history has to be revealed and her secrets told in the general setting-to-rights before the happy-ever-after, though all that this amounted to was that at long last I could bring my car into the garden to stand now where the van stood all those years.

Postscript (1994)

This account of Miss Shepherd condenses some of the many entries to do with her that are scattered through my diaries. Unemphasized in the text (though deducible from the dates of the entries) is the formality of her last days. The Sunday before she died she attended mass, which she had not done for many months; on the Wednesday morning she allowed herself to be taken to be bathed and given clean clothes and then put to bed in the van on clean sheets; and that same night she died. The progression seemed so neat that I felt, when I first wrote it up, that to emphasize it would cast doubt on the truth of my account, or at least make it seem senti-mental or melodramatic. However, the doctor who pro-nounced Miss Shepherd dead said that she had known other deaths in similar circumstances; that it was not (as I had fa-cetiously wondered) the bath that had killed her but that to allow herself to be washed and put into clean clothes was both a preparation and an acknowledgement that death was in the offing.

Nor is it plain from the original account how in the period after her death I got to know the facts of her life that she had so long concealed. A few months before, a bout of flu must have made her think about putting her affairs in or-der and she had shown me an envelope that I might need 'in case anything happens to me, possibly'. I would find the envelope in the place under the banquette where she kept her savings books and other papers. What the envelope contained she did not say, and, when in due course she got over the flu and struggled on, nothing more was said about it.

It was about this time, though, that I had the first and only hint that her name might not be her own. She had, I knew, some money in the Abbey National, and periodically their bright brochures would come through my door—young and happy home-owners pictured gaily striding across their first threshold and entering upon a life of mortgaged bliss.

'Some post, Miss Shepherd,' I would knock on the window and wait for the scrawny hand to come out (nails long and grey; fingers ochre-stained as if she had been handling clay). The brochure would be drawn back into the dim and fetid interior, where it would be a while before it was opened, the packet turned over and over in her dubious hands, the Society's latest exciting offer waiting until she was sure it was not from the IRA. 'Another bomb, possibly. They've heard my views.'

In 1988 the Abbey National were preparing to turn themselves from a building society into a bank, a proposal to which Miss Shepherd for some reason (novelty, possibly) was very much opposed. Before filling in her ballot form, she asked me (and she was careful to couch the question impersonally) if a vote would be valid had the purchaser of the shares changed their name. I said, fairly obviously, that if the shares had been bought in one name then it would be in order to vote in that name. 'Why?' I asked. But I should have known better, and, as so often, having given a teasing hint of some revelation, she refused to follow it up, just shook her head mutely, and snapped shut the window. Except (and this was standard procedure too) as I was passing the van next day her hand came out.

'Mr Bennett. What I said about change of name, don't mention it to anybody. It was just in theory, possibly.'

For some days after Miss Shepherd's death I left the van as it was, not from piety or anything to do with decorum but because I couldn't face getting into it, and though I put on a new padlock I made no attempt to extract her bank books or locate the necessary envelope. But the news had got round, and when one afternoon I came home to find a scrap dealer nosing about I realized I had to grit my teeth (or hold my nose) and go through Miss Shepherd's possessions.

To do the job properly would have required a team of archaeologists. Every surface was covered in layers of old clothes, frocks, blankets and accumulated papers, some of them undisturbed for years and all lying under a crust of ancient talcum powder. Sprinkled impartially over wet slippers, used incontinence pads and half-eaten tins of baked beans, it was of a virulence that supplemented rather than obliterated the distinctive odour of the van. The narrow aisle between the two banks of seats where Miss Shepherd had knelt, prayed and slept was trodden six inches deep in sodden debris, on which lay a top dressing of old food, Mr Kipling cakes, wrinkled apples, rotten oranges and everywhere batteries— batteries loose, batteries in packets, batteries that had split and oozed black gum on to the prehistoric sponge cakes and ubiquitous sherbet lemons that they lay among. A handkerchief round my face, I lifted one of the banquettes where in the hollow beneath she had told me her bank books were hidden. The underside of the seat was alive with moths and maggots, but the books were there, together with other documents she considered valuable: an MoT certificate for her Reliant, long expired; a receipt for some repairs to it done three years before; an offer of a fortnight of sun and sea in the Seychelles that came with some car wax. What there was not was the envelope. So there was nothing for it but to excavate the van, to go through the festering debris in the hope of finding the note she had promised to leave, and with it perhaps her history.

Searching the van, I was not just looking for the envelope; sifting the accumulated refuse of fifteen years, I was hoping for some clue as to what it was that had happened to make Miss Shepherd want to live like this. Except that I kept coming across items that suggested that living 'like this' wasn't all that different from the way people ordinarily lived. There was a set of matching kitchen utensils, for instance— a ladle, a spatula, a masher for potatoes—all of them unused. They were the kind of thing my mother bought and hung up in the kitchen, just for show, while she went on using the battered old-faithfuls kept in the knife drawer. There were boxes of cheap soap and, of course, talcum powder, the cellophane wrapping unbreached; they too had counterparts in the dressing-table drawer at home. Another item my mother hoarded was toilet rolls, and here were a dozen. There was a condiment set, still in its box. When, amid such chaos, can she have hoped to use that particular appurtenance of

gentility? But when did we ever use ours, stuck perma-
nently in the sideboard cupboard in readiness for the social
life my parents never had or ever really wanted? The more I
laboured, the less peculiar the van seemed—its proprieties
and aspirations no different from those with which I had
been brought up.

There was cash here too. In a bag Miss Shepherd carried
round her neck there had been nearly £500, and peeling off
the soggy layers from the van floor I collected about £100
more. Taking into account the money in various building so-
cieties and her National Savings certificates, Miss Shepherd
had managed to save some £6,000. Since she was not entitled to a pension, most of this must have been gleaned from
the meagre allowance she got from the DHSS. I am not sure
whether under the present regime she would have been
praised for her thrift or singled out as a sponger. Arch-Tory
though she was, she seems a prime candidate for Mr Lilley's
little list, a paid-up member of the Something for Nothing
society. I would just like to have seen him tell her so.

Modest though Miss Shepherd's estate was, it was more
than I'd been expecting and made the finding of the envelope
more urgent. So I went through the old clothes again, this
time feeling gingerly in the pockets and shaking out the greasy
blankets in a blizzard of moth and 'French Fern'. But there
was nothing, only her bus-pass, the grim photograph looking
as if it were taken during the siege of Stalingrad and hardly
auguring well for the comedy series she had once suggested I
write on the subject. I was about to give up, having decided
that she must have kept the envelope on her and that it had
been taken away with the body, when I came upon it, stiff

with old soup and tucked into the glove compartment along with another cache of batteries and sherbet lemons, and marked 'Mr Bennett, if necessary'.

Still looking for some explanation ('I am like this, possibly, because . . .'), I opened the envelope. True to form, even in this her final communication Miss Shepherd wasn't prepared to give away any more than she had to. There was just a man's name, which was not her own, and a phone number in Sussex.

I finished cleaning out the van, scraped down the aisle, and opened all the windows and doors so that for the first time since she had moved in it was almost sweet-smelling— only not, because sweet in an awful way was how she had made it smell. My neighbour, the artist David Gentleman, who ten years before had done a lightning sketch of Miss Shepherd watching the removal of an earlier van, now came and did a romantic drawing of this her last vehicle, the grass growing high around it and the tattered curtains blowing in the spring breeze.

2 May 1989

This afternoon comes a rather dapper salvage man who, fifteen years ago, refused to execute a council order for the removal of one of Miss Shepherd's earlier vans on the grounds that someone was living in it. So he says anyway, though it's perhaps just to establish his claim. He stands there on the doorstep, maybe waiting to see if I am going to mention a price; I wait too, wondering if he is going to mention a charge.

Silence on both sides seems to indicate that the transaction is over with no payment on either side, and within the hour he is back with his lifting-gear. Tom M. takes photographs as the van is hauled like an elephant's carcass through the gate and up the ramp, the miraculous tyres still happily inflated; the salvage man scrawls 'On Tow' in the thick dirt on the windscreen; stood by the bonnet I pose for a final photograph (which doesn't come out); and the van goes off for the last time up the Crescent, leaving the drive feeling as wide and empty as the Piazza San Marco.

5 May 1989

'Mr Bennett?' The voice is a touch military and quite sharp, though with no accent to speak of and nothing to indicate this is a man who must be over eighty. 'You've sent me a letter about a Miss Shepherd, who seems to have died in your drive. I have to tell you I have no knowledge of such a person.' A bit nonplussed, I describe Miss Shepherd and her circumstances and give her date of birth. There is a slight pause.

'Yes. Well it's obviously my sister.'

He tells me her history and how, returning from Africa just after the war, he found her persecuting their mother, telling her how wicked she was and what she should and shouldn't eat, the upshot being that he finally had his sister committed to a mental hospital in Hayward's Heath. He gives her subsequent history, or as much of it as he knows, saying that the last time he had seen her was three years ago. He's direct and straightforward and doesn't disguise the fact that he feels guilty about having her committed yet cannot see how he could have done otherwise, how they never got on, and how he cannot see how I have managed to put up with her all these years. I tell him about the money, slightly expecting him to change his tune and stress how close they had really been. But not a bit of it. Since they hadn't got on he wants none of it, saying I should have it. When I disclaim it too, he tells me to give it to charity.

Anna Haycraft (Alice Thomas Ellis) had mentioned Miss S.'s death in her *Spectator* column, and I tell him about this, really to show that his sister did have a place in people's affections and wasn't simply a cantankerous old woman. 'Cantankerous is not the word,' he says, and laughs. I sense a wife there, and after I put the phone down I imagine them mulling over the call.

I mull it over too, wondering at the bold life she has had and how it contrasts with my own timid way of going on—living, as Camus said, slightly the opposite of expressing. And I see how the location of Miss Shepherd and the van in front but to the side of where I write is the location of most of the stuff I write about; that too is to the side and never what faces me.

Over a year later, finding myself near the village in Sussex where Mr F. lived, I telephoned and asked if I could call. In the meantime I'd written about Miss Shepherd in the *London Review of Books* and broadcast a series of talks about her on Radio 4.

17 June 1990

Mr and Mrs F. live in a little bungalow in a modern estate just off the main road. I suppose it was because of the un-hesitating fashion in which he'd turned down her legacy that I was expecting something grander; in fact Mrs F. is disabled and their circumstances are obviously quite modest, which makes his refusal more creditable than I'd thought. From his phone manner I'd been expecting someone brisk and busi-nesslike, but he's a plumpish, jolly man, and both he and his wife are full of laughs. They give me some lovely cake, which he's baked (Mrs F. being crippled with arthritis) and then patiently answer my questions.

The most interesting revelation is that as a girl Miss S. was a talented pianist and had studied in Paris under Cor-tot, who had told her she should have a concert career. Her decision to become a nun put an end to the piano, 'and that can't have helped her state of mind,' says Mr F.

He recalls her occasional visits, when she would never come in by the front door but lope across the field at the back of the house and climb over the fence. She never took any notice of Mrs F., suspecting, rightly, that women were likely to be less tolerant of her than men.

He says all the fiancé stuff, which came via the nuns, is nonsense; she had no interest in men, and never had. When she was in the ambulance service she used to be ribbed by the other drivers, who asked her once why she had never married. She drew herself up and said, 'Because I've never found the man who could satisfy me.' Mystified by their laughter she went home and told her mother, who laughed too.

Mr F. has made no secret of the situation to his friends, particularly since the broadcasts, and keeps telling people he's spent his life trying to make his mark and here she is, having lived like a tramp, more famous than he'll ever be. But he talks about his career in Africa, how he still works as a part-time vet, and I come away thinking what an admirable pair they are, funny and kind and as good in practice as she was in theory—the brother Martha to his sister's Mary.

Sometimes now hearing a van door I think, 'There's Miss Shepherd,' instinctively looking up to see what outfit she's wearing this morning. But the oil patch that marked the site of the van has long since gone, and the flecks of yellow paint on the pavement have all but faded. She has left a more permanent legacy, though, and not only to me. Like diphtheria and Brylcreem, I associate moths with the forties, and until Miss Shepherd took up residence in the drive I thought them firmly confined to the past. But just as it was clothes in which the plague was reputedly spread to the Derbyshire village of Eyam so it was a bundle of Miss Shepherd's clothes, for all they were firmly done up in a black plastic bag, that brought the plague to my house, spreading from the bag to the wardrobe and from the wardrobe to the carpets, the appearance of a moth the signal for frantic clapping and savage stamping. On her death my vigorous cleaning of the van broadcast the plague more widely, so that now many of my neighbours have come to share in this unwanted legacy.

Her grave in the St Pancras Cemetery is scarcely less commodious than the narrow space she slept in the previous twenty years. It is unmarked, but I think as someone so reluctant to admit her name or divulge any information about herself, she would not have been displeased by that.

The Laying On of Hands

SEATED OBSCURELY TOWARDS THE BACK of the church and on a side aisle, Treacher was conscious nevertheless of being much looked at. Tall, thin and with a disagreeable expression, were this a film written forty years ago he would have been played by the actor Raymond Huntley who, not unvinegary in life, in art made a speciality of ill-tempered businessmen and officious civil servants. Treacher was neither but he, too, was nothing to look at. Yet several times he caught women (and it was women particularly) bending forward in their seats to get a better view of him across the aisle; a murmured remark passed between a couple in front, the woman then turning round, ostensibly to take in the architecture but actually to look at him, whereas others in the congregation dispensed with such polite circumspection and just stared.

Unwelcome enough in any circumstances, this scrutiny

was not at all what Treacher had had in mind when he had come into the church fully half an hour before the service was due to start, a precaution against having his hand shaken at the door by the vicar. Such redundant clerical conviviality was always distasteful to Treacher but on this occasion he had a particular reason for avoiding it. Luckily the vicar was not to be seen but, early as he was, Treacher had still had to run the gauntlet of a woman in the porch, a reporter presumably, who was making a record of those attending the memorial service. She held out her book for him to sign.

'Name and organisation?'

But Treacher had pushed past as if she were a lowlier form of autograph hunter. 'Not important,' he said, though whether he meant he was not important or that it was not important his name be recorded was not plain.

'I'll put you under "and many other friends",' she had called after him, though in fact he had never met the deceased and did not even know his name.

Somewhere out of the way was what he wanted, where he could see and not be seen and well back on the side aisle he thought he had found it, instead of which the fuller the church became the more he seemed the focus of attention. It was very vexing.

In fact no one was looking at Treacher at all, except when they pretended to look at him in order also to take in someone sitting in the row behind. A worldlier man than Treacher, if worldliness consists in watching television, would have known why. Seated behind him was a thick-set shaven-headed young man in dark glasses, black suit and black T-shirt who, minus the shades and occasionally (and far too rarely some viewers felt) minus the T-shirt, appeared nightly on the nation's screens in a television soap. The previous week he had stunned his audience when, with no excuse whatsoever, he had raped his mother, and though it later transpired she had been begging for it for some time and was actually no relation at all, nevertheless some vestiges of the nation's fascinated revulsion still clung to him. In life, though, as he was at pains to point out to any chat-show host who would listen, he was a pussy-cat and indeed, within minutes of the maternal rape, he could be found on another channel picking out the three items of antique furniture he would invest in were his budget limited to £500.

None of this Treacher knew, only becoming aware of the young man when an usher spotted him and insisted on shepherding the modest hunk to a more prominent seat off the centre aisle next to a chef who, though famously disgruntled in the workplace, now smilingly shifts along to accommodate the big-thighed newcomer. After his departure Treacher was relieved, though not unpuzzled, to find himself invisible once more and so able to look unobserved at the incoming congregation.

There was quite a throng, with people still crowding through the door and a small queue now stretching over the worn and greasy gravestones that paved this London churchyard. The flanks of the queue were harried by autograph hunters and the occasional photographer, outlying celebrities meekly signing as they shuffled on towards the door. One or two did refuse, on the justifiable grounds that this wasn't a first night (and more of a closing than an opening), but the autograph hunters were impatient of such scruples, considering themselves wilfully thwarted. 'Choosy cow,' one muttered as he turned away from some glacial TV newsreader, brightening only when he spotted an ageing disc jockey he had thought long since dead.

The huddled column pressed on up the steps.

As memorial services go these days it had been billed as 'a celebration', the marrying of the valedictory with the festive convenient on several grounds. For a start it made grief less obligatory, which was useful as the person to be celebrated had been dead some time and tears would have been something of an acting job. To call it a celebration also allowed the congregation to dress up not down, so that though the millinery might be more muted, one could have been forgiven, thought Treacher, for thinking this was a wedding not a wake.

Clive Dunlop, the dead man, was quite young—34 according to the dates given on the front of the Order of Service, though there were some in the congregation who had thought him even younger. Still, it was a shocking age to die, there was no disagreement about that and what little conviviality there might have been was muffled accordingly.

Knowing the deceased, many of those filing into the church in surprisingly large numbers also knew each other, though in the circumstances prevailing at funerals and memorial services this is not always easy to tell as recognition tends to be kept to a minimum—the eye downcast, the smile on hold, any display of pleasure at the encounter or even shared grief postponed until the business of the service is done—however sad the professionally buoyant clergyman will generally assure the congregation that that business is not going to be.

True, there were a number of extravagant one-word embraces, 'Bless!' for instance, and even 'Why?', a despairing invocation that seemed more appropriate for the actual interment which (though nobody seemed quite to know where) appeared to have taken place some six months previously. Extravagant expressions of sorrow seemed out of place here, if only because a memorial service, as the clergyman will generally insist, is a positive occasion, the negative side of the business (though they seldom come out baldly with this) over and done with at the disposal of the body. Because, however upbeat a priest manages to be (and indeed his creed requires him to be), it's hard not to feel that cheerful though the memorial service can be, the actual interment does tend to be a bit of a downer.

Still, discreet funerals and extravagant memorial services are not unusual these days, the finality of death mitigated by staggering it over two stages. 'Of course there'll be a memorial service,' people say, excusing their non-attendance at the emotionally more demanding (and socially less enjoyable) obsequies. And it is generally the case nowadays that anybody who is anybody is accorded a memorial service—and sometimes an anybody who isn't.

Hard to say what Clive was, for instance, though taking note of the numerous celebrities who were still filing in, 'well-connected' would undoubtedly describe him.

Dubbing such a service a celebration was, thought Treacher, a mistake as it could be thought to license a degree of whoopee. The Order of Service included a saxophone solo, which was ominous, and Treacher's misgivings were confirmed when a young man sat down heavily in the pew in front, laid his Order of Service on the ledge then put his cigarettes and lighter beside it.

She was in the next pew, but spotting the cigarettes the spirits of a recently ennobled novelist rose. 'You can smoke,' she whispered.

Her companion shook her head. 'I don't think so.'

'I see no signs saying not. Is that one?'

Fumbling for her spectacles she peered at a plaque affixed to a pillar.

'I think,' said her friend, 'that's one of the Stations of the Cross.'

'Really? Well I'm sure I saw an ashtray as I was coming in.'

'That was holy water.'

In the light of these accessories, more often to be met with in Roman Catholic establishments, it was hardly surprising if some of the congregation were in doubt as to the church's denomination, which was actually Anglican, though a bit on the high side.

'I can smell incense,' said a feared TV interviewer to his actress friend. 'Are we in a Catholic church?'

She had once stabbed a priest to death in a film involving John Mills so knew about churches. 'Yes,' she said firmly.

At which point a plumpish man in a cassock crossed the chancel in order to collect a book from a pew, bowing to the altar en route.

'See that,' said the interviewer. 'The bowing? That's part of the drill. Though it looks a bit pick'n' mix to me. Mind you, that's the trend these days. Ecumenicalism. I talked to the Pope about it once. Sweet man.'

'I missed the funeral,' whispered one woman to her vaguely known neighbour. 'I didn't even know it had happened.'

'Same with me,' the neighbour whispered back. 'I think it was private. What did he die of?'

The sight of a prominent actor in the Royal Shakespeare Company gliding humbly to an empty place in the front row curtailed further discussion, though it was the prototype of several similar conversations going on in various parts of the church. Other people were trying to recall why it was they had failed to attend a funeral which ought to have been high on their lists. Was it in the provinces they wondered, which would account for it, or one of the obscurer parts of South London . . . Sydenham, say, or Catford, venues that would be a real test of anybody's friendship?

It had actually been in Peru, a fact known to very few people in the congregation though in the subdued hum of conversation that preceded the start of the service this news and the unease it generated began to spread. Perhaps out of tact the question 'What did he die of?' was not much asked and when it was sometimes prompted a quizzical look suggesting it was a question best left unput; that, or a sad smile implying Clive had succumbed not to any particular ailment but to the general tragedy that is life itself.

Spoken or unspoken, the uncertain circumstances of the death, its remote location and the shocking prematureness of it contributed to an atmosphere of gloom and, indeed, apprehension in the church. There was conversation but it was desultory and subdued; many people's thoughts seemed to be on themselves. Few of them attended a place of worship with any regularity, their only contact with churches occasions like this, which, as was ruefully remarked in several places in the congregation, 'seemed to be happening all too often these days'.

To Treacher, glancing at the details on the front of the Order of Service it was all fairly plain. He was a single man who had died young. Thirty-four. These days there was not much mystery about that.

'He told me 30, the scamp,' said one of the many smart women who was craning round to see who was still coming in. 'But then he would.'

'I thought he was younger,' said someone else. 'But he looked after himself.'

'Not well enough,' said her husband, whose wife's grief had surprised him. 'I never understood where the money came from.'

Anyone looking at the congregation and its celebrity assortment could be forgiven for thinking that Clive had been a social creature. This wasn't altogether true and this numinous gathering studded with household names was less a manifestation of his friendships than an advertisement for his discretion.

It was true that many of those present knew each other and virtually all of them knew Clive. But that the others knew Clive not all of them knew and only woke up to the fact when they had settled in their seats and started looking round. So while most memorial services take place in an atmosphere of suppressed recognition and reunion to this one was added an element of surprise, many of those present having come along on the assumption they would be among a select few.

Finding this was far from the case the surprise was not untinged with irritation. Or as a go-for-the-throat Australian wordsmith put it to her companion, 'Why, the two-faced pisshole.'

Diffidence was much to the fore. A leading international architect, one of whose airports had recently sprung a leak, came down the centre aisle, waiting at the end of a pew until someone made room, his self-effacing behaviour and downcast eyes proclaiming him a person of some consequence humbled by the circumstances in which he currently found himself and which might have been allegorically represented on a ceiling, say (although not one of his), as Fame deferring to Mortality. 'Do not recognise me,' his look said. 'I am here only to grieve.'

Actually, compared with the soap-stars he hardly counted as famous at all. The world of celebrity in England, at any rate, is small. Whereas fame in America vaults over the barriers of class and profession, lawyers rubbing shoulders with musicians, politicians and stars of the stage and screen, in England, television apart, celebrity comes in compartments, Who's Who not always the best guide to who's who. Thus here Fame did not always recognise Reputation or Beauty Merit.

A high official in the Treasury, for instance, had got himself seated next to a woman who kept consulting her powder compact, her renown as bubbling gameshow host as wasted on him as his skill in succinct summation was lost on her. Worlds collided but with no impact at all, so while what few

lawyers there were knew the politicians and some of the civil
servants, none of them knew the genial wag who pounced
on reluctant volunteers and teased out their less than shame-
faced confessions on late-night TV. The small-screen gardeners knew the big-screen heart-throbs but none of them
recognised 'someone high up in the Bank of England' ('and
I don't mean the window-cleaner,' whispered a man who did).

Much noticed, though, was a pop singer who had been
known to wear a frock but was today dressed in a suit of
stunning sobriety, relieved only by a diamond clasp that had
once belonged to Catherine the Great and which was accompanied by an obligatory security guard insisted on by the
insurance company. This bovine young man lounged in the
pew picking his fingers, happy already to have pinpointed
Suspect No. I, the Waynflete Professor of Moral Philosophy
in the University of Oxford who, timid though he was, clearly
had villain written all over him.

In front of the Professor was a member of the Govern-
ment, who was startled to find himself opposite his Permanent Secretary, seated on the other side of the aisle.

'I didn't know you knew Dunlop,' the minister said the
next day as they plodded through some meeting on carbon
monoxide emissions.

'Oh, I knew him from way back,' said the civil servant
airily.

'Me too,' said the minister. 'Way back.'

Actually the minister had only met Clive quite recently,
just after he became a minister in fact, but this 'way back' in
which both of them took refuge was a time so remote and
unspecific that anything that might have happened then was

implicitly excused by their youth and the temper of the times. 'I knew him in the Sixties' would have been the same, except that Clive was too young for that.

'At some point,' murmured the minister, 'I want you to take me on one side and explain to me the difference between carbon monoxide and carbon dioxide. Fairly star-studded, wasn't it?'

It was, indeed, a remarkable assembly with philanthropy, scholarship and genuine distinction represented alongside much that was tawdry and merely fashionable, so that with only a little licence this stellar, but tarnished throng might, for all its shortcomings, be taken as a version of England.

And 'a very English occasion' was how it was described by the reporter in the *Telegraph* the next day. Not that she was in a position to know as she hadn't bothered to stay for the service. Currently taking down the names of the last few stragglers she compiled her list, procured a programme of the proceedings, then went off to the Design Museum to lunch with a colleague.

'After all,' she said over oeufs en gêlée, 'they're all the same these occasions. Like sad cocktail parties without the drinks.'

This one as it turned out wasn't, so she got the sack. But it was a nice lunch.

Also thinking how English these occasions tended to be was the young priest in charge, Father Geoffrey Jolliffe. Father Jolliffe was Anglican but with Romish inclinations that were not so much doctrinal as ceremonial and certainly sartorial. Amiable, gregarious and plump, he looked well in the cloak he generally went about in, a priest with a bit of a swish to him. His first curacy had been in a slum parish where, as he put it, 'They like a bit of that,' and since he did too, his ministry got off to a good start and that he chose to call the Eucharist 'Mass' and himself 'Father' troubled no one. His present parish, St Andrew Upchance on the borders of Shoreditch and the City, was also poor, but he had done a good deal to 'turn it round', an achievement that had not gone unnoticed in the diocese, where he was spoken of as a coming man.

There were, it is true, some of his fellow clergy who found him altogether too much, but as he said himself, 'There's not enough of "too much" these days,' and since he was a lively preacher and old-fashioned when it came to the prayer book, a large and loyal congregation seemed to bear this out.

Used at his normal services to women predominating, today Father Jolliffe was not altogether surprised to find so many men turning up. Some of them had been close to Clive, obviously, but that apart, in his experience men needed less cajoling to attend funerals and memorial services than they did normal church (or even the theatre, say) and since men seldom do what they don't want, it had made him wonder why. He decided that where the dead were involved there was always an element of condescension: the deceased had been put in his or her place, namely the grave, and however lavish the tributes with which this was accompanied there was no altering the fact that the situation of the living was altogether superior and to men, in particular, that seemed to appeal.

Usually cheerful and expansive, today Father Jolliffe was pre-occupied. He had known Clive himself, which accounted for his church being the somewhat out of the way venue for the memorial service. His death had come as an unpleasant surprise, as, like so many in the congregation, he had not known Clive was even ill. It was sad, too, of course, 'a shared sadness' as he planned to say, but for him, as for others in the congregation, it was somewhat worrying also (though he had no plans to say that).

Still, if he was anxious he did not intend to let it affect his performance. 'And,' as he had recently insisted to a Diocesan Selection Board, 'a service is a performance. Devout, sincere and given wholeheartedly for God, but a performance nevertheless.'

The Board, on the whole, had been impressed.

By coincidence the subject of memorial services had come up at the Board when Father Jolliffe, suppressing a fastidious shudder, had heard himself describe such occasions as 'a challenge'. Urged to expand he had shared his vision of the church packed with unaccustomed worshippers come together, as they thought, simply to commemorate a loved one but also (though they might not know it) hungering for that hope and reassurance which it was the clergy's job to satisfy. This, too, had gone down well with the Board though most of them, Father Jolliffe included, knew it was tosh.

The truth was memorial services were a bugger. For all its shortcomings in the way of numbers a regular congregation was in church because it wanted to be or at least felt it ought to be. It's true that looking down from the pulpit on his flock Sunday by Sunday Father Jolliffe sometimes felt that God was not much more than a pastime; that these were churchgoers as some people were pigeon-fanciers or collectors of stamps, gentle, mildly eccentric and hanging on to the end of something. Still, on a scale ranging from fervent piety to mere respectability these regular worshippers were at least like-minded: they had come together to worship God and even with their varying degrees of certainty that there was a God to worship the awkward question of belief seldom arose.

With a memorial service, and a smart one at that, God was an embarrassment and Father Jolliffe was reminded of this when he had his first sight of the congregation. He had left his service book in his stall and nipping across to get it before putting on his robes he was taken aback at the packed and murmuring pews. Few of those attending, he suspected, had on taking their seats bowed their heads in prayer or knew that that was (once anyway) the form. Few would know the hymns, and still fewer the prayers. Yet he was shortly going to have to stand up and ask them to collaborate in the fiction that they all believed in God (or something anyway) and even that there was an after-life. So what he had said to the Board had been right. It was a challenge, the challenge being that most of them would think this an insult to their intelligence.

How Father Jolliffe was going to cope with this dilemma was interesting Treacher. Indeed it was partly what had brought him to St Andrew's on this particular morning. There were various ways round it, the best of which, in Treacher's view, was not to get round it at all; ignore it in fact, a priest retaining more respect if he led the congregation in prayer with neither explanation nor apology, the assumption being that they were all believers and if not, since they were in the house of God, it behoved them to pretend to be so. Taking the uncompromising line, though, meant that it

was hard then for the clergyman to get on those friendly, in-
formal terms with the congregation that such an occasion
seemed to require. Treacher did not see this as a drawback.
A priest himself, although in mufti, getting on friendly terms
with the congregation had never been high on his list.

Father Jolliffe would not have agreed. 'Whatever else it is,'
he had told the Board, 'a congregation is first and foremost an
audience. And I am the stand-up. I must win them over.' It
was another bold-seeming sentiment that had hit the spot,
occasioning some laughter, it's true, but also much sage
nodding, though not, Father Jolliffe had noticed, from Canon
Treacher, who was an archdeacon and not enthusiastic about
congregations in the first place. Treacher (and his fiercely
sharpened pencil) was the only one of the Board who had
made him nervous (the Bishop was a sweetie), so it was a
blessing that on this particular morning, thanks to Canon
Treacher's precautions, the priest remained unaware of his
presence.

The worst tack a priest could adopt at a service such as
this, and a trap Treacher was pretty confident Father Jolliffe
was going to fall into, was to acknowledge at the start that
the congregation (or 'friends' as Treacher had even heard
them called) might not subscribe to the beliefs implicit in the
hymns and prayers but that they should on no account feel
badly about this but instead substitute appropriate sentiments
of their own. ('I believe this stuff but you don't have to.') Since
in Treacher's experience there would be few in the church
with appropriate sentiments still less beliefs to hand, this
meant that if the congregation thought of anything at all
during the prayers (which he doubted) it was just to try and

summon up a picture of the departed sufficient to squeeze out the occasional tear.

Treacher, it has to be said, had some reason for his pessimism. Casting an eye over the Order of Service Treacher noted that in addition to a saxophone solo a fashionable baritone from Covent Garden was down to sing 'Some Enchanted Evening'. With such delights in prospect Father Treacher feared that liturgical rigour would not be high on the list.

What approach he was going to take to the service ('what angle the priest should come at it') Father Jolliffe had not yet decided, though since he was even now being robed in the vestry it might be thought there was not much time. But he had never been methodical, his sermon often no more than a few headings or injunctions to himself on the back of the parish notes: though on this occasion he had not even bothered with that, preferring, as he would have said, to 'wing it'. This was less slipshod than it sounded, as he genuinely believed that in this 'winging' there was an element of the divine. He had never thought it out but felt that the wings were God-sent, an angel's possibly, or another version of 'Thy wings' under the shadow of which he bade the faithful hide Sunday by Sunday.

He slipped out of the vestry and made his way round the outside of the church to join the choir now assembled at the West door. When he had been appointed vicar at St Andrew's processions generally began obscurely at the vestry winding their awkward way round past the pulpit and up the chancel steps. Father Jolliffe felt that this was untheatrical and missing a trick so one of his first innovations was to make the entrance of the choir and clergy bolder and more dramatic, routeing the procession down the centre of the church.

The procession should have been headed and the choir preceded by a crucifer bearing the processional cross (another innovation), but since this was a weekday Leo, the crucifer, had not been able to get time off work. A beefy young man, Leo was a bus driver and Father Jolliffe had always taken quiet pride in that fact and would occasionally cite him at diocesan conferences as a modern update of the calling of the disciples ('Matthew may have been a tax-collector. What's so special about that? Our crucifer happens to be a bus driver'). Though Leo would much have preferred marching down the centre aisle to where he currently was, stuck behind the wheel of a No. 74 inching up Putney High Street, since privatisation religious obligation was no longer accepted as a reason for absence. 'Or believe me, my son,' said the supervisor, 'come Ramadan and our Sikh and Hindu brethren who compose a substantial proportion of the workforce would be up at the mosque when we need them down at the depot. I'm not without religious feeling myself and my sister-in-law was nearly a nun but sorry, no can do.'

Still, what the procession lacked in splendour at the front it made up in dignity at the back, as in addition to Father Jolliffe also attending the service were several other clergymen, one of them indeed a suffragan bishop. None of them was personally known to Father Jolliffe or seemingly to each other, but all were presumably known to Clive. Though got up in all their gear they were not attending in any official capacity (and in the *Telegraph* report of the occasion they would be described as 'robed and in the sanctuary'), but they definitely brought a kick to the rear of the column which was now assembled and waiting to begin its journey towards the chancel.

The organist was meanwhile playing an arrangement of Samuel Barber's *Adagio for Strings* which many in the congregation were enjoying, having been made familiar with the tune from its frequent airings on Classic FM. Seeing no conclusion in the offing Father Jolliffe pressed a button behind a pillar to alert the organist that they were ready to begin. The Barber now came to a sharp and unceremonious close but since random terminations were not unusual on Classic FM, nobody noticed.

Now from somewhere at the back of the church Father Jolliffe's voice rang out, 'Would you stand?' and the church shuffled to its feet. 'We shall sing the first hymn on your Order of Service, "Love Divine All Loves Excelling".'

Once upon a time it would have been enough to announce the hymn and the congregation would have known to stand. Hymns you stand, prayers you kneel. Nowadays it was prayers you sit, hymns you wait and see what other people are going to do. 'Love,' Father Jolliffe reproached himself. 'We must love one another.'

Now the clergy began to follow the choir down the aisle, Father Jolliffe bringing up the rear, singing the hymn without consulting the words, long since off the book and thus free while singing heartily to cast professionally loving glances to right and left, on his pink and generous face an expression of settled benevolence.

He had still not decided how to pitch his opening remarks, trusting even now that something would occur, in some ways the closest he got to faith in God this trust that when it came to the point words would be put into his mouth. As he passed through the worshippers raggedly singing the hymn, Father Jolliffe thought they looked less like a congregation than an audience, smart, worldly and doubtless expecting him to keep God very much on the back burner. He resented this a little, because, though he was a sophisticated priest and too self-forgiving, his faith was real enough, though so supple and riddled with irony that God was no more exempt from censure than the Archbishop of Canterbury (whom he privately referred to as Old Potato-Face). Still, he resented having to tailor his beliefs to his audience and not for the first time wished he was an out and out Catholic where this problem wouldn't arise. One of the many grumbles Father Jolliffe had about the English Reformation was that it was then that feeling had got into the service, so you couldn't get away with just saying the words but had to mean them at the same time.

These thoughts had taken him and the procession to the chancel, where the choir filed into their pews and the spare clergy disposed themselves around, while still leaving the hymn with a couple of verses to run. This gave Father Jolliffe a chance to think about what he ought to say about Clive and what he ought not to say.

Clive had been a masseur; there was no secret about that. It was something he was very good at and his skill transcended mere physical manipulation. Many of his clients attested to a feeling of warmth that seemed to flow through his fingers and for which there was no orthodox physiological explanation. 'He has healing hands' was one way of putting it or (this from the more mystically inclined) 'He has the Touch.'

That Clive was black (though palely so) was thought by some to account for these healing attributes since it meant (despite his having been born and brought up in Bethnal Green) that he was closer to his origins than were his clients and in touch with an ancient wisdom long since lost to them. Never discouraging these mythic speculations Clive himself had no such illusions, though the pouch to which he stripped to carry out the massage was rudimentary enough to call up all sorts of primitive musings.

The heat that his clients felt, though, was not fanciful and as a boy had embarrassed Clive and made him reluctant to touch or be touched. The realisation that what he had was not a burden but a gift was a turning point and that, with his calorific propensities, it could be marketed was another. And so the laying on of hands became for him a way of life.

There was, of course, more. Though Clive was scrupulous never to omit the ceremony of massage, for some it was just the preliminary to a more protracted and intimate encounter and one which might, understandably, cost them a little more. Looking over the crowded church, Father Jolliffe wondered who were here just as grateful patients whose burden of pain Clive had smoothed away and who had come along to commemorate the easing of a different sort of burden, and of the latter how many were as nervous as he was himself about the legacy that the dead man might have left them.

Now as the hymn ended Father Jolliffe said, 'Will you sit?', gave them a moment to settle and then launched into his pre-amble. And straightaway came out with something he had no intention of saying.

'On such occasions as these,' he said, 'a priest will often preface his remarks with an apology, craving the forgiveness of the congregation since they have had the advantage of knowing the deceased whereas he didn't. I make no such apology. I knew Clive and like most of you, I imagine, loved him and valued his friendship—else why are any of us here?'

Treacher, who was not here for that at all, made a neat note on the back of his Order of Service.

Father Jolliffe was amazed at himself. Few people in the congregation were aware he knew Clive and for various rea-sons, one of which was prudence, he hadn't been planning to say that he did. Now he had blurted it out and must make the best of it, though this would be hard as there was so much he could not say.

For the most part Geoffrey (and there are some circum-stances in which it's right he is called Geoffrey and not Father Jolliffe) . . . for the most part Geoffrey was celibate, though he attached no virtue to this, knowing it was not abstinence so much as lack of opportunity that kept him generally unconju-gate; that and a certain timidity where sex was concerned which made him, despite his (mild) moral disapproval, bestow on an enterprising promiscuity such as Clive's an almost he-roic status. No matter that boldness came as naturally to Clive as diffidence did to Geoffrey or that Clive, of course, was much better looking and unburdened by Geoffrey's thoughts of God (and not looking a fool); Geoffrey knew that in what nowadays is called a one-to-one situation he was what he thought of as shy, so that men who weren't shy, such as Clive, seemed to him warriors, their valour, however profligate, more of a virtue than his own timorous drawing back.

Geoffrey had had experience at first hand of how fly Clive could be. En route for lunch together along the Farringdon Road (not a thoroughfare Geoffrey had ever thought of in a carnal context) Clive had intercepted a male glance that Geoffrey had not even noticed and quick as a fish he had darted away leaving Geoffrey to eat alone and return home disconsolate, where Clive duly came by to give an account of his afternoon. True, Clive was not choosy or how else would he have got into bed with Geoffrey himself, episodes so decorous that for Clive they can scarcely have registered as sex at all, though still tactile enough for Geoffrey, on the news of Clive's death, to be filled with unease.

Being of an Anglo-Catholic persuasion Father Jolliffe practised auricular confession, when he would come clean about his predilections, an ordeal that was somewhat diminished by choosing as his confessor a clergyman whom he knew 'had no problem with that' and being of a similar persuasion himself would place it low down in the hierarchy of possible wickedness. With never much to confess on that particular score, now with Clive gone there was going to be even less.

Somebody coughed. The congregation were waiting and though the pause while Father Jolliffe wrestled with what he should and should not say was understood to be one of deep personal remembrance or even a chance to regain control of his feelings, still, there wasn't all day.

Father Jolliffe plunged on and suddenly it all came right. 'We shall be singing some hymns. We shall pray together and there will be readings and some of Clive's favourite music.' Father Jolliffe paused. 'Prayer may seem to some of you an outmoded activity and hymns too, possibly, but that was not what Clive thought. Clive, as I know personally, was always keen to involve himself in the rites and rituals of the church and were he here he would be singing louder and praying harder than anybody.'

Despite the unintentional disclosure of his friendship with Clive, Father Jolliffe was not displeased with how he (or possibly God) had turned it to good account. Using Clive as a way round any misgivings the congregation might have re the religious side of things was a happy thought. It took the curse off the service very nicely and in the shadows behind the pillar Treacher made another note and this time added a tick.

Actually Geoffrey (we are back to Geoffrey again) knew that where Clive's religious inclinations were concerned he was stretching it a bit. Pious he wasn't and his interest in the rites and rituals of the church didn't go much further than the not unfetching young men who were often helping to perform them, Clive reckoning, not always correctly, that what with the ceremony, the incense and the general dressing-up anyone of a religious disposition was, as he put it, 'halfway there already'. He was particularly keen on vestments, though not in any way Father Jolliffe (sorry) could share with the congregation, having once found Clive in the rectory clad only in his underpants trying on cotta and cope.

Father Jolliffe now led the congregation in prayer, asking

them to kneel if they so chose or simply bow their heads so that they could together remember Clive. Heads went down, eyes were closed with only the security guard on the qui vive, scowling across the bowed benches where someone, he felt sure, might be only pretending to pray. At one point he even stood up and turned round lest some wrongdoer might be taking advantage of these unstructured devotions in order to creep up and snatch the clasp. Suspicious, as he put it, 'of this whole prayer thing' he slumped back moodily in his seat as Jolliffe launched into the Collect.

The vicar didn't improvise prayers, Treacher was relieved to note, drawing them from the ample stock of the old prayer book, and saying them briskly and formally as Treacher preferred them to be said. There were few things worse, in Treacher's view, than a priest who gave too much weight to the words of prayers, pausing as if to invest them with heartfelt meaning and thereby impressing the congregation (and himself) with his sincerity. Treacher had even heard the Lord's Prayer delivered in this fashion and found it intolerable and even queasy. But Father Jolliffe, perhaps because of his Catholic leanings, was dry and to the point. 'Say the word, say the word only' seemed to be his motto and Treacher added another tick.

So far, Treacher was bound to admit, Jolliffe was not doing too badly. Even the news of the priest's friendship with the dead man had scarcely counted against him, as the Archdeacon had all along assumed Jolliffe to be homosexual, though without seeing this as a cause for censure or even a necessary obstacle to promotion. Untrammelled by wife or family and with a housekeeper to look after the vicarage

(when there were vicarages to look after), their energies channelled, the sex under wraps, once upon a time homosexuals
had made excellent priests and still could so long as they were
sensible. The homosexuals Treacher preferred were dry, acer-
bic and, of course, unavowed; A. E. Housman the type that
he approved of, minus the poetry, of course, and (though this
was less important) minus the atheism. Nowadays, though,
discretion had been cast aside and it had all gone splashy,
priests feeling in conscience bound to make their proclivities
plain, with even Jolliffe's declaration of friendship for the
dead man a timorous attempt, Treacher felt, to lay his cards
on the table. Which was a mistake, Treacher believing that
a priest should no more declare a sexual preference than he
should a political one. Even so, Treacher reflected, there was
this to be said in Jolliffe's favour that, whatever his shortcomings, he was not she. In Treacher's church there was a place
for she, running the jumble sale, or doing the altar flowers;
a she could even take the plate round or read the lesson. But
there was no place for she at the altar or in the pulpit. So,
give Jolliffe his due: he was not she.

Now the congregation sat and the scheduled part of the service began. The programme had been put together by Pam,
a cheerful woman Clive had known since childhood and who
was now a producer at the BBC, and Derek, his longtime
landlord. Eclectic would be the kindest word to describe it.
Treacher, who had no reason to be kind, thought it looked a
bit of a ragbag.

First up was a well-known actress and star of a current

sitcom who ascends the stairs of the lectern where she reads immaculately a piece about death not really being the end but just like popping next door. It was a regular standard at memorial services and seeing it billed in the programme Treacher had sighed. He believed in death and when he said he believed in God, death was to a large extent what he meant. These days people didn't, or tried not to, always feeling death was unfair, so when they saw it coming to them or their loved ones they made a great song and dance about it.

And these days there was always blame; it was 'down to' someone or other—the school, the doctor, the police—and you must fight back, that was today's philosophy; in the midst of life we are in death was nowadays a counsel for wimps. It didn't used to be like this, he thought. Had it come from America, he wondered. Or Liverpool? Was television to blame? Or Mrs Thatcher? These days he seldom felt well himself but he wasn't complaining. Or perhaps (and here he was trying to be charitable) what was really distasteful was death as leveller. These days people were so anxious to lay hold of anything that marked them out from the rest—the death of their children, for instance, their neglect by hospitals, being fumbled when young or tortured by nuns; even the murder of loved ones would do if it served to single them out. Whereas the good thing about death was that it singled everybody out. It was the one unchanging thing. Treacher smiled.

Father Jolliffe's thoughts were different, though just as wayward and far from Clive. The next reader had a ponytail and Geoffrey found himself wondering at what point in bed the hair was unloosed, shaken out, let down. And by whom?

He thought of the curtain of hair falling across the pillow, the signal, perhaps (in addition to other signals), that the body was now on offer. So again he remembered Clive.

Next up was a pianist, another personal acquaintance who comes to the piano in mittens which he then takes off before playing some Schubert, the performance of which, judging by his expression, seems to cause him exquisite pain but which turns to dark-faced anger as during the final section a police car drives past with its siren going.

And so it goes on, under Father Jolliffe's benevolent eye, poems, readings, a succession of 'turns' really, one of which, though, Treacher is pleased to note, is from St Paul's First Letter to the Corinthians, the passage about love, with Father Jolliffe opting for the King James version using charity. He took time at the start of the reading to explain to the congregation that charity was love and not anything to do with flag days or people in doorways. Or if it was to do with people in doorways that was only one of its meanings.

Treacher would have scorned such condescension and let the congregation make of it what they could but he forbore to mark his card on the point. Still, he would have preferred it if the great rolling cadences of the Authorised Version hadn't been followed by a saxophone rendition of the Dusty Springfield standard, 'You Don't Have to Say You Love Me', a number (and there was no other word for it) that occasioned a round of applause, from which Treacher unsurprisingly abstained.

During the saxophone solo Geoffrey's worries about Clive recurred. What had he died of? He wished he knew for certain. Or not. Geoffrey had been in bed with Clive seldom and so tamely that only someone as inexperienced as Geoffrey would have thought himself at risk at all. But it did happen, he knew that; he wasn't even sure if there was some risk in kissing (though there hadn't been much of that either).

The truth was it was God that Geoffrey didn't trust. Irony was always the deity's strong point and to afflict a transgressor as timid as Geoffrey with such a disproportionate penalty might appeal to the Almighty's sense of cosmic fun. It was unfair to God, he knew, but he'd always felt the deity had a mean side and on one of his reports at theological college his tutor had written, 'Tends to confuse God with Joan Crawford.'

Treacher looked at his watch. One or two of the participants had preceded their contributions with a few words about Clive—Clive as assiduous and imaginative hospital visitor, Clive as holiday companion, Clive as lover of Schubert and dogs. Still, though these had lengthened the proceedings a little, Treacher was relieved to note that they were now on the last item before the final hymn, a rendering by an ancient musical comedy actress of 'darling Ivor's' immortal 'Fly Home, Little Heart'. 'Fly home, Clive,' she prefaced it, 'our thoughts go with you.'

As her quavering soprano drifted through the church, Treacher began to make plans to slip away as unobtrusively as he had arrived. Slightly to the Archdeacon's regret he had to concede that Father Jolliffe had not done too badly. He had kept the service moving and each contribution brief: he had not sold God short and even allowing for the saxophone solo and the old lady currently in full, if tiny, voice it had never ceased to be a church service. Treacher had come along hoping to find Father Jolliffe a bit of a clown and overanxious to please. There had been no evidence of that and he deserved credit. Canon Treacher folded his Order of Service and put it in his pocket. He would nip out during the last hymn.

Father Jolliffe, too, was pleased the service was over in such good time, though he had some regrets. Varied though the contributions had been he didn't feel they had done justice to Clive and his special charm. Nobody had quite captured his character; an opportunity had been missed. Besides, Father Jolliffe (and he can surely be forgiven) was still somewhat starstruck by his glamorous congregation and understandably wanted to hold on to them for just a little longer. They were such a change from his usual attendance who (while just as precious in the sight of God, of course) were drabber and less fun.

So when the old lady finished and was greeted with such sympathetic applause she had to be coaxed from the microphone before she got into an encore, Father Jolliffe on a sudden impulse (with which he subsequently thought God had had something to do) didn't sink to his knees for the final prayers but stood up, moved to the centre of the chancel steps and expressed the hope that anyone with cherished memories of Clive which they would like to share should now feel free to do so. Treacher frowned and fished the Order of Service out of his pocket to check that this was a departure from the published proceedings. Finding that it was and the proceedings had indeed been prolonged he put a large question-mark in the margin.

Father Jolliffe stood on the chancel steps and in the expectant silence the ponderous workings of the clock, fixed on the back wall of the tower, now began to click and whirr preparatory to slowly striking 12. From experience Father Jolliffe knew that these crankings made speech impossible, so hearing those first admonitory clicks he had learned to pause and wait until the ancient mechanism had run its course.

These necessary cessations often had an opportuneness to them, coming at a pause in a prayer, say, or, as today, at a moment of remembrance, just as year by year the coughing and wheezing ushered in the start of the grandest remembrance of all, the Two-Minute Silence. The unorchestrated pauses, though, were generally less weighty than that but were so repeatedly apposite as to have acquired an almost liturgical significance, the whirring of the cogs and the clanking of the wheels serving to charge the moment, as did the ringing of the bell at the elevation of the Host.

In matters of faith Father Jolliffe might be thought a bit of a noodle but however felicitous the pause in question even he didn't quite identify it as the voice of God. Still, if it was not God speaking, sometimes he felt the Almighty was at least clearing his throat, coughing meaningfully as a reminder of his presence. Father Jolliffe could see no harm in the practice of the presence of God being conflated with the sound of the passage of time, though there were also occasions when the clock's timely intervention irritated him, feeling that there was no need sometimes for the deity to

draw attention to himself so obviously. It had something of
St Peter and the cock crowing thrice about it, not an incident Father Jolliffe was particularly fond of as it showed Jesus
up as a bit of an 'I told you so', which on the quiet the priest
felt he sometimes was anyway.

Today, though, the intervention of the clock was useful
in that it gave the congregation a moment or two to dwell
on what they might want to say about Clive and perhaps as
a consequence once 12 had struck people were not slow to
respond.

A man was straightaway on his feet testifying to Clive's
skill and good humour crewing in a transatlantic yacht race
and another to his unsuspected abilities as a gourmet cook,
testimonials greeted with incredulity in some sections of
the congregation ('Clive?') but elsewhere without surprise.
A woman said what a good gardener he was and how he had
gone on to paint her kitchen, while someone from *Woman's
Hour* described him as 'bright-eyed and bushy-tailed' and
evidenced the large congregation as a testimony to Clive's genius for friendship, a genius incidentally that is generally
posthumous and, like 'touching life at many points' (which
Clive was also said to have done), is only found in obituaries.
On the other hand, 'not suffering fools gladly', another staple
of the obituary column, was not said, Clive having suffered
fools as a matter of course as this was partly what he was
paid for.

A Japanese gentleman now stood up and addressed the
congregation in Japanese, a series of emphatic and seemingly
impassioned declarations of which no one, even those lucky
enough to speak Japanese, understood a word, as the acoustics

of the church (designed by Inigo Jones) made it sound like overhearing an argument. Still, whether out of admiration for his boldness in speaking at all or to compensate him for being Japanese and therefore unintelligible, the congregation gave him a round of applause.

He bowed to every corner of the church then sat down, by which time there were already two more people on their feet wanting to have a word. Treacher began to think his estimate of Father Jolliffe to have been wrong. There was no firm hand here and as a woman behind him said, 'It's going on a bit,' the Archdeacon made another adverse note.

Happy to see it go on was a publisher, a portly and pretentious figure who had never met Clive but was there escorting one of his authors (as yet unennobled), a woman with several bestsellers under her belt but whose work had recently taken a feminist turn and who he feared might be looking for a publisher to match. Coming along to the service just as a chore he had been amazed at the level and variety of celebrity represented and, in the way of publishers, began to scent a book. As more and more of the congregation stood up and the reminiscences about Clive accumulated the publisher grew steadily more excited, occasionally clutching his companion's arm or, like Treacher (but not), scribbling notes on the back of his Order of Service. He saw the book as quick and easy to produce, a tape-recording job largely, a collage of interviews each no more than two or three paragraphs long—a book for people who preferred newspapers and which read like gossip while masquerading as sociology. 'A portrait of a generation'.

Her affection for Clive notwithstanding the novelist

found it hard to reciprocate the publisher's enthusiasm, her own work never having generated a comparable degree of fervour. A woman would understand. As the publisher jotted down the names of possible writers she determined to take her next book where it would be better appreciated. She yawned.

Others were yawning too. Now an elderly couple got up and left, followed a few minutes later by a younger man, tapping his watch, portraying helplessness and mouthing 'Sorry' to an unidentified friend in one of the pews behind.

Father Jolliffe was now wishing he'd never let the congregation off the leash. They were popping up all over the place, never fewer than two people on their feet waiting their turn. Some didn't stand but put a hand up, one of the most persistent a drab youth in an anorak sitting towards the front on the aisle. How he had come to know Clive Father Jolliffe could not imagine.

As a woman ended some protracted hymn to Clive's 'nurturing touch' Father Jolliffe managed to get in before the next speaker. 'I feel,' he said tentatively, 'that as time's getting on we ought to think about drawing these delightful reminiscences to a close,' a warning word that had the opposite effect to that intended as it galvanised all those who had not yet made up their minds to speak now to try and do so. In particular it made the drab youth start waving his hand as if he were still at school and trying to catch the teacher's eye. He looked as if he was at school, too, in jeans and blue anorak, though he had made some effort to dress up for the occasion by putting on a shirt and tie, the shirt rather too big at the collar and the cuffs almost covering his hands. Father Jolliffe wished he would be more forthright and not wait to be called but just stand up and get on with it like other people were doing, currently a philosopher, well groomed and bronzed from a sabbatical at Berkeley.

'Though we knew his name was Clive,' he was saying, 'we'—his wife sitting beside him smiled—'we called him Max, a name I came to feel suited him well. It's not entirely a nice name, not plain certainly or wholesome. In fact Max, really, is the name of a charmer, implying a degree of sophistication, a veneer of social accomplishment. It's urban, metropolitan, the name of someone who could take a vacant place at a poker game, say, and raise no eyebrows, which someone called . . . oh, Philip, say, couldn't.'

At this a woman in front turned round. 'I called him Philip.' Then turning to her neighbour. 'He said that was what he felt like inside.'

'I called him Bunny,' said a man on the aisle and this was the signal for other names to be tossed around—Toby, Alex and even Denis, all, however unlikely, attested to and personally guaranteed by various members of the congregation—so that still on his feet to bear witness to the unique appropriateness of Max the philosopher begins to feel a bit of a fool and says lamely, 'Well, he was always Max to us but this was obviously a many-sided man . . . which is yet another cause for celebration.' And sits down plumply to a reassuring pat from his wife.

One of the names submitted in contention with Max was Betty, the claims for which had been quite belligerently advanced by a smallish young man in a black suit and shaven head who was sitting towards the front with several other young men similarly suited and shorn, one or two of them with sunglasses lodged on top of their hairless heads.

Now, ignoring the woman whose turn it was and the feebly waving youth, the young man, who gave his name as Carl, addressed the congregation. 'Knowing Clive well I think he would be touched if someone'—he meant himself—'were to say something about him as a lover.'

A couple who had just got up to go straightaway sat down again. There was a hush, then a woman in the front row said: 'Excuse me. Before you do that I think we ought to see if this lady minds.' She indicated her neighbour, a shabby old woman in a battered straw hat, her place also occupied by a couple of greasy shopping bags. 'She might mind. She is Mr Dunlop's aunt.'

Father Jolliffe closed his eyes in despair. It was Miss Wishart and she was not Clive's aunt at all. Well into her eighties and with nothing better to do Miss Wishart came to every funeral or memorial service that took place at the church, which was at least warm and where she could claim to be a distant relative of the deceased, a pretence not hard to maintain as she was genuinely hard of hearing and so could ignore the occasional probing question. Sometimes when she was lucky (and the relatives were stupid) she even got invited back for the funeral tea. All this Father Jolliffe knew and could have said, but it was already too late as Carl was even now sauntering round to the front pew where Miss Wishart was sitting in order to put the question to her directly.

With set face and making no concessions to her age or

sensibilities Carl stood over Miss Wishart. 'Do you mind if we talk about your nephew's sex life?' Her neighbour repeated this in Miss Wishart's ear and while she considered the question, which she heard as having to do with his ex-wife, Carl looked up at Father Jolliffe. 'And you don't object, padre?'

It's often hard these days for the clergy not to think of God as a little old-fashioned and Father Jolliffe was no exception. So if he was going to object it wasn't on grounds of taste or decorum but simply in order to cut the service short. But what he really objected to was the condescension of 'padre' (and even its hint of a sneer) so this made him feel he couldn't object on any grounds at all without the young man thinking he was a ninny.

'No, I've no objection,' he said, 'except'—and he looked boldly down at this small-headed creature—'I think what we're talking about is love. Clive's love life.' Then, thinking that didn't sound right either, 'His life of love.'

That sounded even worse and the young man smirked.

Treacher sighed. Jolliffe had been given an opportunity to put a stop to all this nonsense and he had muffed it. Had he been in charge he would have put the young man in his place, got the congregation on their knees and the service would have been over in five minutes. Now there was no telling what would happen.

As an indication that the proceedings were descending into chaos Treacher noted that one or two men in the congregation now felt relaxed enough to take out mobile phones and carry on hushed conversations, presumably rearranging appointments for which the length of the service was now making them late. The young man in front pocketed his cigarettes and lighter and strolled up the aisle to slip out of the West door where he found that two or three other likeminded smokers had preceded him. They nattered moodily in nicotine's enforced camaraderie before grinding their fags into the gravestones and rejoining the service at the point where the question about her nephew's sex life had at last got through to Miss Wishart and her neighbour was able to announce the verdict to the congregation. 'His aunt doesn't mind.'

There was a smattering of applause to signify approval of such exemplary open-mindedness in one so old, but since the question Miss Wishart thought she'd been asked was not to do with her nephew's sex life but with his next life, her tolerance hadn't really been put to the test.

'I just thought,' said Carl standing on the chancel steps, 'that it would be kind of nice to say what Clive was like in bed?' It was a question but not one that expected an answer. 'I mean, not in detail, obviously, only that he was good? He took his time and without being, you know, mechanical he was really inventive? I want,' he said, 'to take you on a journey? A journey round Clive's body?'

Treacher sank lower in his seat and Geoffrey's smile lost some of its benevolence as Carl did just that, dwelling on each part, genitals for the moment excepted, with the fervour if not quite the language of the metaphysical poets.

Though it was a body Geoffrey was at least acquainted with, Carl's version of it rang no bells and so he was reassured when he saw one or two in the congregation smiling wistfully and shaking their heads as if Carl had missed the point of Clive's body. Still, Geoffrey hoped nobody was going to feel strongly enough about this discrepancy to offer up a rival version as, however fascinating this material was, he felt there was a limit to what the congregation would stand.

'Do we really want to know this?' a senior official in the Foreign Office muttered to his wife (though in truth he knew some of it already and unbeknownst to him, so did she).

Actually Geoffrey was surprised at Carl's forbearance in omitting the penis, an intimate survey of which he was obviously capable of providing did he so choose. Perhaps, Geoffrey thought, he was saving it up but if so it was to no purpose as it was while Carl was en route from the scrotum to the anus that suddenly it all got too much and a man was bold enough to shout out: 'Shame.'

Carl rounded on him fiercely. 'No, there was no shame. No shame then and no shame now. If you didn't understand that about Clive, you shouldn't be here.'

After which, though there were no more interruptions, the congregation felt slightly bullied and so took on a mildly mutinous air.

A woman sitting near to the front and quite close to Carl said almost conversationally: 'And you made this journey quite often, did you?'

'What journey?'

'Round Clive's body.'

'Sure. Why?'

'It's just that, while I may be making a fool of myself here,' and she looked round for support, 'I didn't know he was . . . that way.'

Several women who were within earshot nodded agreement.

'To me he was—' and she knew she was on dangerous ground, 'to me, he wasn't that way at all.'

Carl frowned. 'Do you mean gay?'

The woman (she was a buyer for Marks and Spencer's) smiled kindly and nodded.

'Well let me tell you,' said Carl, 'he was "that way".'

Though these exchanges are intimate and conversational they filter back through the congregation where they are greeted with varying degrees of astonishment, some of it audible.

'She didn't know?'

'Who's she kidding?'

'Clive,' the woman went on, 'never gave me to suppose that his sexual preferences were other than normal.'

'It is normal,' shouted Carl.

'I apologise. I mean conventional.'

'It's conventional, too.'

'Straight then,' said the buyer with a gesture of defeat. 'Let's say straight.'

'Say what you fucking like,' said Carl, 'only he wasn't. He was gay.'

Smiling and unconvinced she shook her head but said no more.

During this exchange Geoffrey had been thinking about Carl's hair or lack of it, the gleam of his skull through the blond stubble making him look not unlike a piglet. Once upon a time hair as short as this would have been a badge of a malignant disposition, a warning to keep clear, with long hair indicating a corresponding lenity. With its hint of social intransigence it had become a badge of sexual deviance, which it still seemed to be, though nowadays it was also a useful mask for incipient baldness, cutting the hair short a way of pre-empting the process.

'Fucking' had put a stop to these musings though Carl had said it so casually that for all they were in church no one seemed shocked (Treacher fortunately hadn't heard it) and Father Jolliffe decided to let it pass.

In his fencing match with the buyer from M&S Carl had undoubtedly come out on top but it had plainly disconcerted him and though he resumed his journey round Clive's body, when he got to his well-groomed armpits he decided to call it a day. 'When someone dies so young,' he summed up, 'the pity of it and the waste of it touch us all. But when he or she dies of AIDS'—someone in the congregation gave a faint cry—'there should be anger as well as pity, and a resolve to fight this insidious disease and the prejudice it arouses and not to rest until we have a cure.' Carl sat down to be embraced by two of his friends, his stubbly head rubbed by a third.

Hearing AIDS mentioned for the first time and what had hitherto been vague fears and suspicions now given explicit corroboration many in the congregation found it hard to hide their concern, this death which had hitherto been an occasion for sorrow now a cause for alarm.

One woman sobbed openly, comforted by her (slightly pensive) husband.

A man knelt down and prayed, his companion stroking his back gently as he did so.

'I didn't think you needed to die of it anymore,' a round the world yachtswoman whispered to her husband. 'I thought there were drugs.'

Others just sat there stunned, their own fate now prefigured, this memorial service a rehearsal for their own.

One of these, of course, was Father Jolliffe who is professional enough, though, to think this sobering down might be given prayerful expression, all this worry and concern channelled into an invocation not only for Clive but for all the victims of this frightful disease and not merely here but in Africa, Asia and America and so on. The landscape of the petition taking shape in his mind he stood up and faced the congregation. 'Shall we pray.'

As he himself knelt he saw the student-type in the anorak, impervious to the atmosphere obviously, still with his hand up and waving it even more vigorously now. But enough had been said and the priest ignored him.

There is a hush, with Treacher relieved that Father Jolliffe has at last got a grip on the service and is now going to bring these unseemly proceedings to a fitting conclusion.

'Vicar.'

It was the young man in the anorak. His voice was very clear in the silence and those of the congregation who had knelt or just put their heads down now raised them to look and Treacher, who had felt this service could hold no more surprises, said 'Oh God' and would have put his head in his hands had it not been there already.

Even the easy-going Father Jolliffe was taken aback at this unheard-of interruption. 'I was praying,' he said reproach-fully.

He thought the young man blushed but he was looking so worked up it was hard to tell. A long-wristed, narrow-faced, straight-shouldered young man now looking sheep-ish. 'I did have my hand up before,' he said. 'And besides, it's probably relevant to the prayer.'

Had it not come at such an inopportune moment the no-tion that a prayer needed to be up to the minute and take account of all relevant information would have merited some thought and indeed might have provided a useful subject for 'Faith and Time', the series of discussion groups Father Jolliffe was currently running after Evensong on Sundays; the topicality of intercession in the light of the omniscience of God, for instance, or prayers taking place in time and God not. As it was the priest found himself staring at the young man, all pastoral feeling suspended, and saying rather crossly, 'Well?'

'My name is Hopkins,' said the young man. 'I'm on my year out. I'm going to do geology. I was in South America looking at rocks.'

Some of this he said loudly enough for the congregation to hear, but other less relevant remarks he gave almost as an aside to the nearby pews, so that somebody out of range said: 'What?'

'On his year out, doing geology,' somebody else called back.

'And?' said somebody else under their breath.

'I got sponsorship from Tilcon,' the young man added redundantly.

Somebody sighed heavily and said: 'Do we need to know this?'

'That was why I was in Peru. The rocks are very good there.'

'Can't hear,' said a well-known commentator on the arts. 'I know about Peru and even I can't hear.'

A woman nearby smiled kindly at the boy, and indicated he should speak up.

'The thing is'—and the speaking up made him sound defiant—'I was staying in the same hotel as Mr Dunlop when he died, and he didn't die of AIDS.'

Finding him so unprepossessing and with no air of authority whatever (and, it has to be said, younger than most of their children) the congregation were disinclined to give him much attention. What had seemed just another tedious reminiscence is at first listlessly received and it's only when the glad message 'Not AIDS' begins to be passed round and its significance realised that people begin to take notice, some at the back even standing up to get a better view of this unlikely herald.

It takes a little time and to begin with there is some shaking of heads but soon smiles begin to break out, people perk up and this nondescript young man suddenly finds himself addressing an audience that hangs on his every word. 'I know there is nothing to be ashamed of whatever it was he died of, but with all due respect to the person who spoke, who obviously knew him much better than I did, all the same I was there when he died and I'm sure his aunt, at least, would like to know it was not AIDS.'

'HIV-related,' corrected a man with a ponytail.

'Yes, whatever,' says the student.

'It wasn't AIDS,' Miss Wishart's helpful neighbour shouts in her ear. 'Not AIDS.'

Meeting an uncomprehending smile from the old lady, she thinks to mime the condition by pointing to her bottom and shaking her head, thereby causing much offence to Carl and his glabrous colleagues and bringing Miss Wishart no nearer enlightenment. The only aids she has come across are deaf aids and hers plainly isn't working.

Hopkins, having given his welcome news, offers no evidence to back it up and now seems disposed to sit down again except that Father Jolliffe, who, if he had been an MP and addressing the House of Commons, would at this point have had to preface his question by declaring an interest, leans over the lectern and says, 'And do you mind telling us Mr . . . ?'

'Hopkins.'

'Mr Hopkins, do you mind telling us how Mr Dunlop did die?'

The young man blew his nose, carefully wiped it, and put away his handkerchief.

'Well, basically he had been on a trip which took him through some rough country where he was like bitten by some insect or other, you know, the name of which I can't remember, only the doctors at the hospital knew it. He got this fever. He was in the room next door to me at the hotel, to begin with anyway. Then they took him in and that was it basically. I was surprised as it's not a tropical place. The climate's not very different from Sheffield. I come from Sheffield,' he added apologetically.

Hopkins remained on his feet looking round at the congregation and smiling helpfully as if to suggest that if there were any more questions he would be happy to try and answer them. He doesn't have long to wait.

'I do not believe this,' Carl mutters as he gets to his feet though it is not to ask a question. He wholly ignores the student and talks to the church. 'I'm sorry? I thought we'd grown up? I thought we'd learned to look this thing in the face? I never thought I'd still be hearing tales of some ailment picked up in the wilds of Tibet. Or a wasting disease caught from the udders of Nepalese yaks. It's not from a bite. It's not from cat hairs. It's not from poppers nor is it a congenital disease of the dick. It's a virus passed via blood and sex and that's how it's caught. Not from some fucking Peruvian caterpillar. Of course it was AIDS. Look at his life. How could it be anything else?'

In the silence that followed, many look desperately at the student in the hope he has something more to offer by way of rebuttal. But at 19 debate is hardly his strong point. He shrugs awkwardly and sits down shaking his head, long wrists dangling between his knees.

Unpleasant and arrogant though Carl had been, and with a manner seemingly designed to put people's backs up, there were many in the congregation who felt that he was right. They longed passionately to believe in this Peruvian caterpillar and its death-dealing bite. South America was a dangerous place, everyone knew that; there were the pampas, gauchos and regular revolutions. The Maya had perished, so why not

Clive? But what Carl had said made sense. Of course it was AIDS. No one could screw as much as he had done and go unpunished. So the sentence that had been all too briefly remitted was now reimposed and hopes momentarily raised were dashed once more. But to have been given a vision of peace of mind and then to see it snatched away made the burden even harder to bear.

One couple held each other's hands in mute misery. Which had slept with Clive—or both? What did it matter? Never had they been so close.

Still, the couples who had shared Clive's favours were better placed than husbands or wives who had known him singly. 'What does it signify anyway,' said a fierce-eyebrowed judge, who knew Clive only as someone who occasionally unfroze his shoulder. 'He's dead, that's the essence of it.' His wife, who was keeping very quiet, shifted in her seat slightly as she was suffering from thrush, or that was what she hoped.

Symptoms were back generally. A pitiless quiz-show host found herself with a dry mouth. The suffragan bishop knew he had a rash. A stand-up comedian had a cold sore that didn't seem to clear up and which was masked by make-up. Now it had suddenly begun to itch. He had a powder compact but dared not consult it. Those who were famous, though, knew better than to turn a hair. Their anxiety must be kept private and unshown for they were always under scrutiny. They must wait to share their worries discreetly with friends or, if with the general public, at a decent price from the newspapers concerned.

Husbands who thought their wives didn't know, put a face on it (though their wives did know very often). Wives who thought their husbands didn't know (which they generally didn't) masked their distraction in a show of concern for others, one, for instance, patting the shoulder of a man in front who, without looking, took the hand and held it to his cheek.

The congregation had been given a glimpse of peace; the itch had gone, the cough had stilled, the linen was unsoiled; the pores had closed, the pus dried up and the stream ran clear and cool. But that was what it had been, a glimpse only. Now there was to be no healing. There was only faith.

How to put this into prayer. Father Jolliffe clasped his hands and tried once more. 'Shall we pray?'

They settled and waited as he sought for the words.

'May I speak?'

Baulked for a second unbelievable time on the brink of intercession, Father Jolliffe nearly said 'No' (which is what the Archdeacon would have said, who has long since written down: 'Hopeless. Lacks grip.' And now inserts 'totally').

Father Jolliffe searches the congregation to see who it is who has spoken and sees, standing at the back, a tall, distinguished-looking man. 'I am a doctor,' he says.

This is unsurprising because it is just what he looks like. He is dry, kindly-faced and yet another one who doesn't speak up. 'I am a doctor,' he repeats. 'Mr Dunlop's doctor, in fact. While his medical history must, of course, be confidential'— 'Must be what?' somebody says. 'Controversial,' says someone else—'I think I am not breaking any rules when I say that Mr Dunlop was a most . . . ah . . . responsible patient and came to me over a period of years for regular blood tests.'

'Regular blood tests' goes round the pews.

'These were generally a propos HIV, the last one only a

week before his departure for South America. It was negative. What this fever was that he died of I'm in no position to say, but contrary to the assertions made by the gentleman who spoke earlier'—he meant Carl—'it seems to me most unlikely, in fact virtually impossible, that it was HIV-related. Still,' he smiled sadly, 'the fact remains that Clive is dead and I can only offer my condolences to his grieving friends and to his aunt. Whatever it was her nephew died of, her grief must be unchanged.'

Miss Wishart is nudged by her neighbour and when the doctor is pointed out to her, smiles happily and gives him a little wave. She seldom got such a good ride as this.

As the doctor sat down there was a ripple of applause and as the news filtered to the acoustically disadvantaged areas of the church it grew and grew. People at the front stood up and began applauding louder and those further back followed suit until the whole church was on its feet clapping.

'Good old Clive!' someone shouted.

'Trust Clive,' said someone else and there was even some of that overhead clapping and wild whoops that nowadays characterises audiences in a TV studio or at a fashionable first night.

Seldom even at a wedding had the vicar seen so many happy faces, some openly laughing, some weeping even and many of them embracing one another as they were called on to do in the Communion Service, but never with a fervour or a fellow-feeling so unembarrassed as this. It was, thought Father Jolliffe, just as it should be.

Still, it was hard to say what it was they were applauding: Clive for having died of the right thing (or not having died of the wrong one) and for having been so sensible about his blood tests; the young student for having brought home the news; or the urbane-looking doctor for having confirmed it. Father Jolliffe was glad to see that God came in for some of the credit and mindful of the setting one woman sank to her knees in prayer, and both genders got onto their mobiles to relay the news to partners and friends whose concern for themselves (and for Clive, of course) was as keen as those present in the congregation.

Some wept and, seeing the tears, wondering partners took them as tears for Clive. But funeral tears seldom flow for anyone other than the person crying them and so it was here. They cried for Clive, it is true, but they cried for themselves without Clive, particularly now that his clean and uncomplicated death meant that he had thankfully left them with nothing to remember him by.

Amid the general rejoicing even Carl looked a little more cheerful, though it was hard for him to be altogether wholehearted, the dead man just having been dropped from a club of which Carl was still a life member and from which he stood no chance of exclusion. There were one or two others in the same boat and knew it, but they clapped too, and tried to rejoice.

Though his companion the novelist was gratefully weeping, the publisher's thanksgiving was less wholehearted. AIDS never did sales any harm and gave a tragic momentum even to the silliest of lives, whereas it was hard not to think that there was only bathos in a death that resulted from being bitten by a caterpillar. Still, the geology student seemed naive and possibly suggestible, so Clive's death could be made—and moralistically speaking ought to be made—more ambiguous than it really was. Nobody liked someone who had had as much sex as Clive to get off scot free and that included the idle reader. No, there was a book here even so; the absurd death was just a hiccup and smiling too, the publisher joined in the clapping.

But clapping whom? Father Jolliffe decided it might as well be God and raising his voice above the tumult he said: 'Now [and for the third time of asking], shall we pray?' This even got a laugh and there was a last whoop before the congregation settled down. 'Let us in the silence remember our friend Clive, who is dead but is alive again.'

This, however hallowed, was not just a phrase. Clive's imagined death had been baneful and fraught with far-reaching implications so that, devoid of these, his real (and more salubrious) demise did seem almost a resurrection. And in that cumbrous silence, laden with prayers unmouthed, loosed from anxiety and recrimination many do now try and remember him, some frowning as they pray with eyes closed but seeing him still, some open-eyed but unseeing of the present, lost in recollection. In the nature of things, these memories are often inappropriate. Some think, for instance, of what Clive felt like, smelled like, recalling his tenderness and his tact. There was the diligence of his application and pictured in more than one mind's eye was that stern and labouring face rising and falling in the conscientious performance of his professional duties.

'I sing his body,' prayed Geoffrey to himself. 'I sing his marble back, his heavy legs'—he had been reading

Whitman—'I sing the absence of preliminaries, the curt-
ness of desire. Dead, but not ominously so, now I extol him.'

'I elevate him,' thought a choreographer (for whom he had
also made some shelves), 'a son of Job dancing before the
Lord.'

'I dine him,' prayed one of the cooks, 'on quails stuffed
with pears in a redcurrant coulis.'

'I adorn him,' imagined a fashion designer. 'I send him
down the catwalk in chest-revealing tartan tunic and trews
and sporting a tam o'shanter.'

'I appropriate him,' planned the publisher, 'a young man
eaten alive by celebrity' (the dust-jacket Prometheus on the
rock).

None, though, thought of words and how the bedroom
had been Clive's education. It was there that he learned that
words mattered, once having been in bed with an etymologist whose ejaculation had been indefinitely postponed when
Clive (on being asked if he was about to come too) had murmured, 'Hopefully.' In lieu of discharge, the etymologist had
poured his frustrated energy into a short lecture on neolo-
gisms which Clive had taken so much to heart he had never
said 'hopefully' again.

Nothing surprised him, nothing shocked him. He was
not—the word nowadays would be judgmental, but Clive
knew that there were some who disliked this word, too, and
preferred censorious, but he was not judgmental of that
either.

Words mattered and so did names. He knew if someone
disliked their name and did not want it said, still less called

out, during lovemaking. He knew, too, his clients' various names for the private parts and what he or she preferred to call them and what they preferred him to call them (which was not always the same thing). He knew, too, in the heightened atmosphere of the bedroom how swiftly a misappellation in this regard could puncture desire and shrivel its manifestation.

He brought to the bedroom a power of recall and a grasp of detail that would have taken him to the top of any profession he had chosen to enter. A man who could after several months' interval recall which breast his client preferred caressed could have run the National Theatre or reformed the Stock Exchange. He knew what stories to whisper and when not to tell stories at all and knew, too, when the business was over, never to make reference to what had been said.

Put simply this was a man who had learned never to strike a false note. He was a professional.

Aloud Geoffrey said: 'Let us magnify him before the Lord. O all ye works of the Lord, bless ye the Lord: praise him and magnify him forever.'

Geoffrey rose to his feet. 'And now we end this service of thanksgiving with John Keble's hymn.'

New every morning is the love . . .
Our waking and uprising prove
Through sleep and darkness safely brought
Restored to life and power and thought.

How glumly they had come into the church and how happily now, their burden laid down, do they prepare to go forth. So they sing this mild little hymn as the chorus sings their deliverance in *Fidelio,* or the crowd sings at Elland Road. They sing, distasteful though that spectacle often is, as they sing at the Last Night of the Proms. And singing they are full of new resolve.

Since the news of Clive's death a shadow had fallen across sexual intercourse. Coming together had become wary, the whole business perfunctory and self-serving, and even new relationships had been entered on gingerly. As one wife, not in the know, had complained, 'There is no giving anymore.' In some bedrooms where intercourse had not been wholly discontinued prophylactics had appeared for the first time, variously explained by a trivial infection or a sudden sensitivity, but in all cases made out to the unknowing partner as just a minor precaution not the membrane between life and death.

Now that time of sexual austerity was over. This was the liberation, and many of the couples pressing out of the door looked forward to resuming all those sexually sophisticated manoeuvres that Clive's death and its presumed cause had seen discontinued.

Partners not in the know were taken aback by the gusto with which their long-diffident opposites now went to it, and some, to put it plainly, could scarcely wait to get home in order to have a fuck. And indeed some didn't, one couple sneaking round behind the church to the alcove outside the vestry that sheltered the dustbins and doing it there. They happened both to be friends of Clive and so of the same mind, but several husbands, ignorant of their wives' connection with the dead man, were startled to find themselves unexpectedly fingered and fondled (evidence of the strong tide of relief that was sweeping their partners along) and one, made to park on a double yellow line in the Goswell Road, had to spread a copy of the *Financial Times* over his knees while beneath it his wife gave vent to her euphoria.

For some, though, deliverance would be all too brief. A TV designer, a particular friend of Clive and thus feeling himself more enshadowed than most, was so rapturous at the news of Clive's unportentous death that he celebrated by picking up a dubious young man in Covent Garden, spending a delightful evening and an unprotected night, waking the next morning as anxious as he had been before and in much the same boat.

Still, others thought they had learned their lesson and crowding up the aisles they saw the West door open on a churchyard now bathed in sunlight. The bells were ringing out; the vicar was there shaking hands; truly this had been a thanksgiving and an ending and now the portals were flung open on a new life.

'I presume he had us all on his computer somewhere,' someone said.

'Who cares?' said someone else.

Slowly they shuffled towards the light.

It was now well past lunchtime and the Archdeacon had stomach ache. Anxious to get away before the crowd and unobserved by the vicar, who would surely be shaking all those famous hands, Canon Treacher had got up smartly after the blessing only to find his exit from the pew blocked by a woman doing what she (and Canon Treacher) had been brought up to do, namely, on entering or leaving a church to say a private prayer. It was all Treacher could do not to step over her, but instead waited there fuming while she placidly prayed. She took her time with God, and then, her devotions ended, more time assembling her umbrella, gloves and what she called apologetically 'my bits and bobs' and then when she was finally ready, had to turn back to retrieve her Order of Service, which she held up at Canon Treacher with a brave smile as if to signify that this had been a job well done. By which time, of course, the aisle was clogged with people and Treacher found himself carried slowly but inexorably towards the door where, as he had feared, Father Jolliffe was now busy shaking hands.

Even so, the priest was so deep in conversation with a leading chat-show host that Treacher thought he was going to manage to sidle by unnoticed. Except that then the priest saw him and the chat-show host, used to calling the shots with regard to when conversations began and ended, was startled to find this chat abruptly wound up as Jolliffe hastened across to shake Treacher's cold, withdrawing hand.

'Archdeacon. What a pleasure to see you. Did you know Clive?'

'Who? Certainly not. How should I know him?'

'He touched life at many points.'

It was a joke but Treacher did not smile.

'Not at this one.'

'And did you enjoy the service?' Father Jolliffe's plump face was full of pathetic hope.

Treacher smiled thinly but did not yield. 'It was . . . interesting.'

With Father Jolliffe cringing under the archidiaconal disapproval it ought to have been a chilling moment and, by Treacher at least, savoured and briefly enjoyed, but it was muffed when the hostess of a rapid response TV cookery show, whom the vicar did not know, suddenly flung her arms round his neck saying, 'Oh, pumpkin!'

Firm in the culinary grasp, Father Jolliffe gazed helplessly as the Archdeacon was borne away on the slow-moving tide and out into the chattering churchyard where, holy ground notwithstanding, Treacher noted that many of the congregation were already feverishly lighting up.

When, a few days later, Treacher delivered his report, it was not favourable, which saddened the Bishop (who had, though it's of no relevance, been a great hurdler in his day). Rather mischievously he asked Treacher if he had nevertheless managed to enjoy the service.

'I thought it,' said Treacher, 'a useful lesson in the necessity for ritual. Or at any rate, form. Ritual is a road, a path between hedges, a track along which the priest leads his congregation.'

'Yes,' said the Bishop, who had been here before.

'Leave the gate open, nay tell them it's open as this foolish young man did, and straightaway they're through it, trampling everything underfoot.'

'You make the congregation sound like cattle, Arthur.'

'No, not cattle, Bishop. Sheep, a metaphor for which there is some well-known authority in Scripture. It was a scrum. A free-for-all.'

'Yes,' said the Bishop. 'Still,' he smiled wistfully, 'that

gardening girl, the footballer who's always so polite—I quite wish I'd been there.'

Treacher, feeling unwell, now passes out of this narrative, though with more sympathy and indeed regret than his acerbities might seem to warrant. Though he had disapproved of the memorial service and its altogether too heartfelt antics he is not entirely to be deplored, standing in this tale for dignity, formality and self-restraint.

Less feeling was what Treacher wanted, the services of the church, as he saw it, a refuge from the prevailing sloppiness. As opportunities multiplied for the display of sentiment in public and on television—confessing, grieving and giving way to anger, and always with a ready access to tears—so it seemed to Treacher that there was needed a place for dryness and self-control and this was the church. It was not a popular view and he sometimes felt that he had much in common with a Jesuit priest on the run in Elizabethan England—clandestine, subversive and holding to the old faith, even though the tenets of that faith, discretion, understatement and respect for tradition, might seem more suited to tailoring than they did to religion.

Once out of the churchyard the Archdeacon lit up, his smoking further evidence that there was more to this man than has been told in this tale. There had briefly been a Mrs Treacher, a nice woman but she had died. He would die soon, too, and the Bishop at least would be relieved.

Back at the church, Geoffrey was shaking hands to the finish, with last out, as always, Miss Wishart who was still attesting her supposed connection with the deceased. 'Somebody said something about drinks for my nephew. Where would they be? A sherry was what he preferred only I like wine.'

The priest pointed her vaguely in the direction of the churchyard which with people standing about talking and laughing looked like a cocktail party anyway. He had been asked to drinks himself by a florid and effusive character, a publisher apparently, with a stonyfaced woman in tow. He had taken both Geoffrey's hands warmly in his, saying he had this brilliant idea for a book and he wanted to run it past him.

This, taken with the upbeat conclusion of the service, ought to have cheered him, but Father Jolliffe found himself despondent. The presence of the Archdeacon could only mean one thing: he had been vetted. For what he wasn't sure, but for promotion certainly. And equally certainly he had failed to impress. For a start he should not have invited the congregation to participate. He knew that from something that had happened at the Board, when in answer to a question about the kiss of peace and the degree of conviviality acceptable at the Eucharist, he had said that the priest was, in a real sense, the master of ceremonies. This had got a laugh from the Board (the Bishop actually guffawing), except that he had noticed that Treacher was smiling in a different way and making one of his spidery notes: he was not impressed then and he had not been impressed now.

Still, had he not, as it were, thrown the service open to the floor, the true circumstances of Clive's death would never have emerged so he could not regret that. What the Lord giveth the Lord also taketh away. He went back into the now empty church to get out of his gear.

'Should I have spoken?' Hopkins was still slumped in his pew. Now he got up clutching his backpack in front of him like a shield. 'I wondered if it was out of turn.'

'Not at all,' said Geoffrey, noticing that the young man had loosened the unaccustomed tie and undone the top button of his shirt, so that he looked younger still and not so old-fashioned. It was difficult to think of him at Clive's death-bed.

'You did the right thing, Mr Hopkins. There were many people'—he didn't say himself—'who were grateful. It lifted a burden.'

The boy sat down again cradling his backpack. 'The young guy seemed pretty pissed off. The—' he hesitated, 'the gay one?'

Hopkins had an unconvincing earring that Geoffrey had not spotted, ear and earring now briefly caught in a shaft of light, a faint fuzz on the fresh pink ear.

'People were upset,' Geoffrey said. 'Clive was . . . well, Clive.' He smiled, but the young man still looked unhappy.

'I felt a fool.' He sat hugging his backpack then suddenly brightened up. 'That blonde from *EastEnders* was on my row. Clive never told me he knew her.'

Geoffrey thought that there were probably quite a few things Clive had never told him and wondered if anything had happened between them. Probably not, if only because he imagined there was more on offer in South America and the local talent doubtless more exotic.

He was an awkward boy with big hands. He was the kind of youth Modigliani painted and for a moment Geoffrey wondered if he was attractive, but decided he was just young.

'And that cook who slags people off? He was here too.'

'Yes,' said Geoffrey. 'It was a good turn-out.' Then, feeling he ought to be getting on. 'They're all outside.'

The youth did not notice the hint still less take it. 'You said you knew Clive?'

'Yes,' said Geoffrey, then added, 'but not well.'

'I'd never seen anybody die before. It was depressing?'

Geoffrey smiled sadly and nodded as if this were an aspect of death that had not occurred to him. The youth was a fool.

'Can I show you something?' The student rooted in his pack then put it on the floor so that the priest could sit beside him. 'I had to go through his stuff after he died. There wasn't much. He was travelling light. Only there was this.'

It was a maroon notebook, long, cloth-covered and meant to fit easily into a pocket. Geoffrey thought he remembered it and ran his hand over the smooth, soft cover.

'Is it a diary?' the priest said.

'Not exactly.'

In the churchyard the party was beginning to break up. One group had arranged to lunch at the Garrick and were moving round saying their farewells while someone looked for a cab. Others were going off to investigate a new restaurant that had opened in a converted public lavatory and of which they'd heard good reports, though tempted to join forces with yet another party who were venturing into one of the last genuine cafés patronised by the porters at Smithfield where the tripe was said to be delicious.

Most of the big stars had left pretty promptly, their cars handily waiting nearby to shield them from too much unmediated attention. The pop star's limo dropped him first then called at the bank so that the security guard could redeposit the clasp and then took him on to a laboratory in Hounslow where, as a change from Catherine the Great, he was mounting vigil over some hamsters testing lip-gloss. Meanwhile, the autograph hunters moved among what was left of the congregation, picking up what dregs of celebrity that remained.

'Are you anybody?' a woman said to the partner of a soap-star, 'or are you just with him?'

'He was my nephew,' said Miss Wishart to anyone who would listen.

'Who, dear?' said one of the photographers, which of course Miss Wishart didn't hear, but she looked so forlorn he took her picture anyway, which was fortunate, as he was later able to submit it to the National Portrait Gallery where it duly featured in an exhibition alongside the stage doorman of the Haymarket and the maitre d' of the Ivy as one of 'The Faces of London'.

Soon, though, it began to spit with rain and within a few minutes the churchyard was empty and after its brief bout of celebrity, back to looking as dingy and desolate as it generally did.

'No it isn't a diary,' said Hopkins. 'It's more of an account book.'

It was divided into columns across the page, each column numbered, possibly indicating a week or a month, the broad left-hand column a list of initials, and in the other columns figures, possibly amounts. The figures were closely packed and as neat as the work of a professional accountant.

'Can you make it out?' said the young man, running his finger down the left-hand column. 'These are people, I take it.'

'They might be,' said Geoffrey. 'I don't quite know.' Having just spotted his own initials, Geoffrey knew only too well, though he noted that the spaces opposite his own name were only occasionally filled in. This was because Clive came round quite spasmodically and wasn't often available when Geoffrey called (now, seeing the number of people on his list, he could see why). When he did come round the visit did not always involve sex ('No funny business' is how Clive put it). Geoffrey told himself that this was because he was a clergyman and that he thus enjoyed a relationship with Clive that was pastoral as well as physical. More often than not this meant he found himself making Clive scrambled eggs, while Clive lay on the sofa watching TV in his underpants, which was about as close to domesticity as Geoffrey ever got. Still, Geoffrey had always insisted on paying for this privilege (hence the entries in the notebook), though really in order to give credence to the fiction that sex wasn't what their friendship was about. Though, since he was paying for it, it wasn't about friendship either, but that managed to be overlooked.

'Did you see a lot of each other? In Peru?'

Geoffrey was anxious to turn the page and get away from those incriminating initials.

'Yes. We had meals together quite often. I could never figure out what he was doing there.'

'What did you eat?' said Geoffrey. 'Eggs?'

'Beans, mostly. He said he was travelling round. Seeing the world.'

As casually as he could Geoffrey turned the page.

'These figures,' said Hopkins, turning it back. 'What do you think they mean?'

'They're on this page, too,' said Geoffrey turning the page again. 'And here,' turning another.

Hopkins blew his nose, wiped it carefully and put the handkerchief away. 'Is it sex, do you think?'

'Sex?' said Geoffrey with apparent surprise. 'Why should it be sex?' He looked at Hopkins as if the insinuation were his and almost felt sorry for him when the young geologist blushed.

'Clive was a masseur. They may be payments on account—if they're payments at all. I think when he was hard up at one period he used to provide home help, carpentry and so on. It could be that.'

'Yes? You say he was a masseur. He told me he was a writer.'

Geoffrey smiled and shook his head.

'My guess is that it's a sort of diary and I don't feel,' Geoffrey said pompously, 'that one ought to read other people's diaries, do you?'

Hopkins shrank still further and Geoffrey hated himself.

He went on leafing through. Against some of the names were small hieroglyphics that seemed to denote a sexual preference or practice, an indication of a client's predilections possibly, of which one or two were obvious. Lips with a line through, for instance, must mean the person with the initials didn't like being kissed; lips with a tick the reverse. But what did a drawing of a foot indicate? Or an ear? Or (in one case) two ears?

None of the drawings was in any sense obscene and were so small and symbolic as to be uninteresting in themselves, but what they stood for—with sometimes a line-up of three or four symbols in a row—was both puzzling and intriguing.

It was a shock, therefore, for Geoffrey to turn the page and come across a note en clair that was both direct and naive:

Palaces I have done it in:
Westminster
Lambeth
Blenheim
Buckingham (2)
Windsor

Except Windsor was crossed out with a note, 'Not a palace,' and an arrow led from Westminster to a bubble saying 'Lost count'. Written down baldly like this it seemed so childish and unsophisticated as not to be like Clive at all, though as notes for a book, Geoffrey could see it made some sort of sense.

'It's rather sad, really,' Geoffrey went on, still in his

pompous mode. 'Why bother to write it down? Who'd be interested?'

'Oh, I keep notes myself,' said Hopkins. Then, as the priest looked up, startled, 'Oh, not about that. Just on rocks and stuff. He told me he was writing a book, but people do say that, don't they? Particularly in South America.'

It's true Clive had spoken of writing a book, or at least of being able to write a book, 'I could write a book,' often how he ended an account of some outrageous escapade. Geoffrey may even have said, 'Why don't you?' though without ever dreaming he would.

Like many who hankered after art, though, Clive was saving it up, if not quite for a rainy day at least until the right opportunity presented itself—prison perhaps, a long illness or a spell in the back of beyond. Which, of course, Peru was and which was why, Geoffrey presumed, he had taken along the book.

Still, he wasn't sure. Clive was always so discreet and even when telling some sexual tale he seldom mentioned names and certainly not the kind of names represented at the memorial service. This iron discretion was, Clive knew, one of his selling points and part of his credit, so not an asset he was likely to squander. Or not yet anyway.

Hopkins seemed to be taking less interest in the diary and when Geoffrey closed the book and put it on the pew between them the young man did not pick it up but just sat staring into space.

Then: 'Of course, if it is sex and those are initials and you could identify them it would be dynamite.'

'Well, a mild sort of dynamite,' said Geoffrey, 'and only if a person,' Geoffrey smiled at the young man, 'only if a person was planning to reveal information . . .' He left the sentence unfinished. 'And that would, of course, be . . .' and he left this sentence unfinished too, except at that moment a police car blared past outside. Geoffrey sighed. God could be so unsubtle sometimes. 'Besides,' he went on, 'if this is entirely about sex, and I'm not sure it is, it's not against the law is it?' He wondered how long he could get away with reckoning to be so stupid.

Having found someone, as he thought, more ingenuous than himself the young man was determined to instruct him in the ways of the world. 'No,' he said patiently, 'but it would make a story. Several stories probably. Stories for which newspapers would pay a lot of money.'

'You wouldn't do that, surely?'

'I wouldn't, but someone might.' Hopkins picked up the book. 'I wondered about handing it over to the police.'

'The police?' Geoffrey found himself suddenly angry at the boy's foolishness. 'What for?'

'For safe-keeping?'

'Safe-keeping,' shouted Geoffrey, all pretence of naivety gone. 'Safe-keeping? In which case why bother with the police at all. Just cut out the middleman and give it to the *News of the World*?'

Taken aback by this unexpected outburst Hopkins looked even more unhappy. 'I don't know,' he said, nuzzling his chin on top of his pack. 'I just want to do the right thing.'

The right thing to do was nothing but Geoffrey did not

say so. Instead he thought of all the people behind the initials, the troubled novelists, the tearful gardeners and stone-
faced soap-stars, Clive's celebrity clientele dragged one by
one into the sneering, pitiless light. Something had to be
done.

He put his hand on the young man's knee.

He felt Hopkins flinch but kept his hand where he had
put it, or not where he had put it, he decided subsequently,
but where God had put it. Because tame and timid though
such a move might seem (and to someone of Clive's sophistication, for instance, nonchalant and almost instinctive), for
Geoffrey it was momentous, fraught with risk and the dread
of embarrassment. He had never made such a bold gesture
in his life and now he had done it without thinking and
almost without feeling.

The young man was unprepossessing and altogether too
awkward and angular; in the street he would not have looked
at him twice. But there was his hand on the boy's knee. 'What
is your name?' he said.

'Greg,' Hopkins said faintly. 'It's Greg.'

Geoffrey had no thought that the presence of his hand
on the young man's knee would be the slightest bit welcome
nor, judging by the look of panic on his face, was it. Greg
was transfixed.

'I am wondering, Greg,' said Geoffrey, 'if we are getting
this right. We are talking about what to do with this notebook when strictly speaking, legally speaking'—he squeezed
the knee slightly—'it has got nothing to do with us anyway.'

'No?'

'No. The notebook belongs after all, to Clive. And now to his estate. And whom does his estate belong to . . . or will do eventually?'

Hopkins shook his head.

'His only surviving relative. Miss Wishart!'

The priest loosened his grip on the knee, though lingering there for a moment as it might be preparatory to travelling further up the young man's leg. This galvanised Hopkins and he got up suddenly. Except that the priest got up too, both crammed together in the close confinement of the pew, the priest seemingly unperturbed and never leaving his face his kind, professional, priestly smile.

Hopkins was now unwise enough to put his hand on the edge of the pew. Geoffrey promptly put his hand on top of it.

'No, no,' said Hopkins.

'No what?' said Geoffrey kindly.

'No, she should keep the book.' Hopkins pulled his hand away in order to retrieve the book still lying on the seat. 'Where can I find her?'

'She comes to church. I can give it to her.' Geoffrey reached for the book and fearful that he was reaching for him too, Hopkins relinquished it without a struggle.

'I can give it to her as a relic of her nephew. The only relic really.' He stroked the book fondly and in that instant Hopkins was out of the pew and on his way to the door. But not quickly enough to avoid the priest's kindly hand pressing into the small of his back and carrying with it the awful possibility that it might move lower down.

'Yes,' Hopkins said, 'give it to her. She's the person.' And stopping suddenly in order to put on his backpack he got rid of the hand, but then found it resting even more horribly on his midriff, so that he gave a hoarse involuntary cry before the priest lifted his hand with a bland smile, converting the gesture almost into a benediction.

'Won't she be shocked?' Hopkins said as he settled the pack on his back. 'She's an old lady.'

'No,' said Geoffrey firmly. 'And I say this, Greg, as her parish priest. It's true she's an old person but I have found the old are quite hard to shock. It's the young one has to be careful with. They are the prudes nowadays.'

Hopkins nodded. Irony and geology obviously did not mix.

'I wondered if you wanted a cup of tea?' Geoffrey stroked the side of his backpack.

'No,' he said hurriedly. 'No, I've got to be somewhere.'

Still widely smiling Geoffrey put out his hand.

They shook hands and the young man dashed out of the door and quickly across the wet gravestones, Geoffrey noting as he did so that he had that overlong and slightly bouncy stride he had always associated with flute-players, train-spotters and other such unworldly and unattractive creatures.

Something strange, though, now happened that Geoffrey would later come to see as prophetic. Or at least ominous. The boy had pulled out a knitted cap and as he stopped to put it on he saw the priest still standing there. Suddenly and unexpectedly the boy smiled and raised his hand. 'I'm sorry,' he called out, and then about to go, he stopped again. 'But thank you all the same.'

Geoffrey sat down in the nearest pew. He was trembling. After a bit he got up and went into the vestry where he opened the safe in which was kept the parish plate, the chalice (Schofield of London, 1782) and the two patens (Forbes of Bristol, 1718), each in its velvet-lined case. On the shelf below them Geoffrey put Clive's book.

Over the following weeks Geoffrey would often open up the safe and take a peek at the book, trying to decipher Clive's cryptography and gauge the extent and nature of his activities. None of it shocked him: indeed he found the exercise vaguely exciting and as near to pornography as he allowed himself to come.

Whether it was thanks to the book or to that almost involuntary pass that had allowed him to retain it Geoffrey found his life changing. Disappointed of immediate promotion he was now more . . . well, relaxed and though 'Relax!' is hardly at the core of the Christian message he did feel himself better for it.

So it might be because he was easier with himself or that his unique pass at the geology student had broken his duck and given him more nerve but one way and another he found himself having the occasional fling, in particular with the bus-driving crucifer, who, married though he was, didn't see that as a problem. Nor did Geoffrey's confessor who, while absolving him of what sin there was, urged him to see this and any similar experiences less as deviations from the straight and narrow and more as part of a learning curve. In fairness, this wasn't an expression Geoffrey much cared for, though he didn't demur. He preferred to think of it, if only to himself, as grace.

He still kept the book in the safe, though, as it represented a valorous life he would have liked to lead and still found exciting. It happened that he had been to confession the day before and just as a diabetic whose blood tests have been encouraging sneaks a forbidden pastry so he felt he deserved a treat and went along to the church meaning to take out Clive's book. It was partly to revisit his memory but also because even though he now knew its mysterious notations by heart they still gave him a faint erotic thrill. He knew that this was pathetic and could have told it to no one, except perhaps Clive, and it was one of the ways he missed him.

Pushing open the door of the church he saw someone sitting towards the front and on the side. It was the geology student, slumped in the same pew he had sat in at the memorial service.

'Hail,' said the young man. 'We meet again.' Geoffrey shook hands.

'I meant to come before now,' he said, 'only my car's not been well.'

Geoffrey managed a smile. Seeing him again, Geoffrey thought how fortunate it was that his advance had been rejected. God had been kind. It would never have done.

Hopkins made room for Geoffrey to sit down, just as he had on the first occasion they had talked.

'I came back,' he said, as if it were only that morning he had fled the church. 'I thought about it and I thought, why not?' And now he turned towards Geoffrey and looking him sternly in the eye put his hand on the vicar's knee. 'All right?'

Geoffrey did not speak.

There was a click, then another and the turning of a wheel and faintly, as if from a great way off, Geoffrey heard the cogs begin to grind as the clock gathered itself up and struck the hour.

Father! Father! Burning Bright

ON THE MANY OCCASIONS Midgley had killed his father, death had always come easily. He died promptly, painlessly and without a struggle. Looking back, Midgley could see that even in these imagined deaths he had failed his father. It was not like him to die like that. Nor did he.

The timing was good, Midgley acknowledged that. Only his father would have managed to stage his farewell in the middle of a 'Meet The Parents' week. It was not a function Midgley enjoyed. Each year he was dismayed how young the parents had grown, the youth of fathers in particular. Most sported at least one tattoo, with ears and noses now routinely studded. Midgley saw where so many of his pupils got it from. One father wore a swastika necklace, of the sort Midgley had wondered if he felt justified in confiscating from a boy. And a mother he had talked to had had green hair. 'Not just green,' muttered Miss Tunstall, 'bright green. And then you wonder the girls get pregnant.'

That was the real point of these get-togethers. The teachers were appalled by the parents but found their shortcomings reassuring. With parents like these, they reasoned, who could blame the schools? The parents, recalling their own teachers as figures of dignity and authority, found the staff sloppy. Awe never entered into it, apparently. 'Too human by half' was their verdict. So both Nature and Nurture came away, if not satisfied, at any rate absolved. 'Do you wonder?' said the teachers, looking at the parents. 'They get it at school,' said the parents.

'Coretta's bin havin' these massive monthlies. Believe me, Mr Midgley, I en never seen menstruatin' like it.' Mrs Azakwale was explaining her daughter's poor showing in Use of English. 'She bin wadin' about in blood to her ankles, Mr Midgley. I en never out of the launderette.' Behind Mrs Azakwale, Mr Horsfall listened openly and with unconcealed scepticism, shaking his head slowly as Midgley caught his eye. Behind Mr Horsfall, Mr Patel beamed with embarrassment as the large black woman said these terrible things so loudly. And beyond Mr Patel, Midgley saw the chairs were empty.

Mrs Azakwale took Coretta's blood-stained track record over to the queue marked Computer Sciences, leaving Midgley faced with Mr Horsfall and Martin.

Mr Horsfall did not dye his hair nor wear an earring. His hair was now fashionably short but only because he had never got round to wearing it fashionably long. Nor had his son Martin ever ventured under the drier; his ears, too, were intact. Mr Horsfall was a detective sergeant.

'I teach Martin English, Mr Horsfall,' said Midgley, wishing he had not written 'Hopeless' on Martin's report, a document now gripped by Mr Horsfall in his terrible policeman's hand.

'Martin? Is that what you call him?'

'But that's his name.' Midgley had a moment of wild anxiety that it wasn't, that the father would accuse him of not even knowing the name of his son.

'His name's Horsfall. Martin is what we call him, his mother and me. For your purposes I should have thought his name was Horsfall. Are you married?'

'Yes.'

Horsfall was not impressed. He had spent long vigils in public toilets as a young constable. Many of the patrons had turned out to be married and some of them teachers. Marriage involved no medical examination, no questionnaire to speak of. Marriage for these people was just the bush they hid behind.

'What does my son call you?'

'He calls me Mr Midgley.'

'Doesn't he call you sir?'

'On occasion.'

'Schools . . .' Horsfall sniffed.

His son ought to have been small, nervous and bright, Midgley the understanding schoolteacher taking his part against his big, overbearing parent. He would have put books into his hands, watched him flower so that in time to come the boy would look back and think 'Had it not been for him . . .' Such myths sustained Midgley when he woke in the small hours of the morning and drowsed during the middle period of the afternoon. But they were myths. Martin was large and dull. He was not unhappy. He would not flower. He was not even embarrassed. He was probably on his father's side, thought Midgley, as he sat there looking at his large inherited hands, and occasionally picked at one of a scattering of violet-painted warts.

'What worries me,' said Horsfall, 'is that he can scarcely put two words together.'

This was particularly hurtful to a man who, in his professional capacity, specialised in converting the faltering confessions of semi-illiterates into his plain policeman's prose. He could do it. At four o'clock in the morning after a day spent combing copses and dragging ponds, never mind house-to-house enquiries, he could do it. Why not his son?

'You show me up, Martin, having to come along here. I don't grudge coming along here. But what I would like to have come along here as is a proud father. To be told of your achievements. Be shown your name in gilt letters on the honours board. Martin Horsfall. But no. What is it? It's Geography: Poor. History: Poor. English: Hopeless. PE: Only fair. Why Martin?

'Why, Mr Midgley? And why hopeless? Geography: Poor. History: Poor. English: Hopeless. Is he hopeless or are you?'

'He doesn't try.'

'Do you challenge him? We challenge him at home. His mother and I challenge him. Does he get challenged at school? I don't see it.' Horsfall looked round but caught the eye of Mr Patel, who was smiling in anticipation of his interview. Mr Patel's son was clever. Blacks, Indians. That was why. Challenge. How could there be any challenge?

'I never had chances like he had. And I dare say you didn't. We never had chances like that, Martin.'

At the 'we' Midgley flinched, suddenly finding himself handcuffed to Horsfall in the same personal pronoun.

'A school like this. Modern buildings. Light. Air. Sporting facilities tip-top. Volleyball. If somebody had come up to me when I was your age and said "There are facilities for volleyball", I would have gone down on my knees. What do you say?'

The question Horsfall was asking his son had no obvious answer. Indeed, it was not really a question at all. 'Justify your life'; that was what this dull and dirty youth was being asked to do. Not seeing that justification was necessary, the son was silent and the father waited.

And it was in the middle of this silence that Miss Tunstall came up to say the hospital had telephoned. Except that, sensing this was not simply a silence but an essential part of what was being said, she did not immediately interrupt but made little wavings with her hand behind Mr Horsfall's head, who—a policeman and ever on the watch for mockery—turned round. So it was to him that Miss Tunstall gave the bad news (a man in any case used to transactions with ambulances, hospitals and all the regimes of crisis).

'The hospital's just rung. Mr Midgley's father's been taken ill.' And only then, having delivered her message did she look at Midgley, who thus heard his father was dying at second-hand and then only as a kind of apology.

'They're ringing the ward,' said Midgley. 'It's a fall, apparently.' One ear was in Miss Tunstall's office, the other fifty miles away in some nowhere behind a switchboard.

'You want to pray it's not his hip,' said Miss Tunstall.

'That's generally the weak spot.' She had a mother of her own. 'The pelvis heals in no time, surprisingly.' She did not sound surprised. Her mother had broken her pelvis and she had thought it was the beginning of the end. 'No. It's when it's the hip it's complicated.'

'Switchboard's on the blink,' said a voice.

'Join the club,' said another. 'I've been on the blink all day.'

'It's the dreaded lurgi,' said the first voice.

'Hello,' said Midgley. But there was silence.

'She took a nasty tumble in Safeway's last week,' went on Miss Tunstall. 'They do when they get older. It's what you must expect.' She expected it all the time. 'Their bones get brittle.'

She cracked her fingers and adjusted the spacing.

'Maintenance,' said a new voice.

'I've been wrongly connected,' said Midgley.

'It's these ancillary workers,' said Miss Tunstall. 'Holding the country to ransom. Other people's suffering is their bread and butter.' She was wanting to get on with a notice about some boys acting the goat in the swimming baths but felt she ought to wait until Midgley had heard one way or the other. Her mother was 82. The last twenty years had not been easy and had she known what was in store she thought now she would probably have stabbed her mother to death the second she turned 60. These days it would only have meant a suspended sentence or if the worst came to the worst open prison. Miss Tunstall had once been round such an institution with the school and found it not uncongenial. A picnic in fact.

'Records are on the warpath again,' said a voice in Midgley's ear.

'It never rains,' said another.

'Should I be sterilisin' this?' said a black voice.

'Search me, dear,' said an emancipated one.

'Hello,' said Midgley. 'HELLO.'

Softly Miss Tunstall began to type.

Midgley thought of his father lying in bed, dying but not wanting to be any trouble.

'No joy?' said Miss Tunstall, uncertain whether it would be better to underline 'the likelihood of a serious accident'. 'And then they wonder why people are stampeding to BUPA.'

Midgley decided he had been forgotten then a crisp voice suddenly said 'Sister Tudor'.

'I'm calling about a patient, a Mr Midgley.'

Noiselessly Miss Tunstall added an exclamation mark to 'This hooliganism must now STOP!' and waited, her hands spread over the keys.

'What is the patient's name?'

'Midgley,' said Midgley. 'He came in this morning.'

'When was he admitted?'

'This morning.'

'Midgley.' There was a pause. 'We have no Midgley. No Midgley has been admitted here. Are you sure you have the right ward?'

'He was admitted this morning. I was told he was seriously ill.'

'Oh yes.' Her tone changed. 'Midgley. What is your name?'

'Midgley.'

'Are you next of kin?'

'My father is dead,' he thought. 'Only the dead have next of kin.'

'I'm his son.'

Miss Tunstall folded her hands in her lap.

'He's not at all well.' The tone was reproachful rather than sympathetic. 'We think he's had a stroke. He's been lying on the floor. He ought to have been in hospital sooner. There's now the question of pneumonia. It's touch and go.'

'It's touch and go,' said Midgley, putting the phone down.

'How old is he?' said Miss Tunstall, noticing she had typed 'tooling' for 'fooling'.

'He's 74.'

Her mother was 82. She ripped out the paper and wound in another sheet. Life was unfair.

The door opened.

'Been on the phone again, Midgley?' said the headmaster. 'I'm the one who has to go cap in hand to the Finance Committee.'

'Mr Midgley's father's ill,' said Miss Tunstall, once again the apologetic herald. 'Apparently it's touch and go.'

And she started typing like the wind.

'Of course you can go. Of course you must go. One's father. There can be no question. A filial obligation.' Midgley was in the headmaster's study. 'It's awkward, of course. But then it always is.' It was death. It was a reshuffling of the timetable.

Midgley's thoughts were with his father in Intensive Care.

'Was he getting on in years?'

No effort was being spared to keep him alive and in the present and yet grammatically he kept slipping into the past.

'He's 74.'

'Seventy-four. Once upon a time I thought that was old. You won't be gone long? What, three, four days?' In his mind the headmaster roughed out a timetable whereby Midgley senior could decently die, be buried and Midgley junior be back in harness. Radical surgery on the timetable might still be avoided.

'Let me see. It's English, Integrated Humanities and Creative Arts, nothing else, is there?'

'Environmental Studies.'

The headmaster groaned. 'That's the awkward one. Pilbeam's off on another course. That's the trouble with the environment, it involves going on courses. I'll be glad when the environment is confined to the textbooks.'

'Ah well,' said the headmaster. 'It can't be helped.' He had never understood the fuss people made about their parents. 'Both of mine were despatched years ago. A flying bomb.' He made it sound like a victory for common sense.

'He must have fallen and not been able to get up,' said Midgley. 'He was lying there two days.'

'An all too familiar scenario these days,' said the headmaster. 'Isolated within the community. Alone in the crowd. You must not feel guilty.'

'I generally go over at weekends,' said Midgley.

'It will give Tomlinson an opportunity to do some of his weird and wonderful permutations with the timetable. Though I fear this one will tax even Tomlinson's talents.'

The headmaster opened the door.

'One must hope it is not as grave as it appears. One must hope he turns the corner. Corners seem to have gone out of medicine nowadays. In the old days the sick were always turning them. Illness is now much more of a straight road. Why is that?'

It was not a question he wanted answering.

'Antibiotics?' said Midgley, lingering.

'Sometimes one has the impression modern medicine encourages patients to loiter.' It was Midgley who was taking his time.

'Mistakenly, one feels. Godspeed.'

Miss Tunstall had finished the notice about acting the goat in the swimming baths and the headmaster now glanced through it, taking out his pen. She made a start on another notice about the bringing of pupils' cars to school, one of the head's 'privilege not a right' notices. Midgley still hesitated.

'I'm not sure if we've couched this in strong enough terms, Daphne.'

'It's as you dictated it.'

'I have no doubt. But I feel more strongly about it now. Nothing else is there, Midgley?'

Midgley shook his head and went out.

'A boy slips. Is pushed and we are talking about concussion. A broken neck. A fatality, Daphne. I intend to nail the culprits. I want them to know they will be crucified.'

'Shall I put that?'

The headmaster looked at her sharply and wondered if Miss Tunstall was through the menopause.

'We must find a paraphrase. But first the problems caused

by this business of Midgley père. Ask Tomlinson to step over, will you, Daphne. Tell him to bring his coloured pencils. And a rubber.'

'Tomato or my jam?'

'Tomato.'

The hospital was fifty miles away. His wife was making him sandwiches. He sat in his raincoat at the kitchen table, watching her apply a faint smear of Flora to the wholemeal bread.

'I wanted to go over this last weekend,' said Midgley. 'I would have gone over if your Margaret hadn't suddenly descended.'

'You knew they were coming. They'd been coming for weeks. It's one of the few things Mother's got to look forward to.' Mrs Midgley's mother was stood staring out of the window. 'Don't blame our Margaret.'

'I just never expected it,' said Midgley.

If you expected something it didn't happen.

'I expected it,' said his wife, putting on a shiny plastic apron emblazoned with a portrait of Sylvia Plath.

'I expected it. Last time I went over he came to the door to wave me off. He's never done that before. Bless him.' She slipped on a pair of padded Union Jack mittens and sinking to her knees before the oven gave the Shift a trial blast. 'I think people know.'

'He does come to the door,' said Midgley. 'He always comes to the door.' And it was true he did, but only, Midgley felt, to show that the visit had been so short it needed extending. Though once, catching sight of him in the rear-view mirror, waving, Midgley had cried.

'He was trying to tell me something,' said his wife.

'I know a farewell when I see one.' A fine spray misted the oven's pale grey walls. 'Shouldn't you be going?'

'Is it Saturday today?' said her mother.

Ten minutes later Midgley was sitting on the stairs and his wife had started hoovering.

'I'm not going to let him down. I want to be there when he goes,' shouted Midgley.

The vacuum was switched off.

'What?'

'He loved me.'

'I can't think why,' said Midgley's wife. 'It's not as if you take after him,' and she switched on again, 'not one little bit.'

'Joyce,' her mother called, 'when is that chiropodist coming?'

Midgley looked at his watch. It was three o'clock. At ten past Mrs Midgley took to dusting. It was always assumed the housework put her in a bad temper. The truth was if she was in a bad temper she did the housework. So it came to the same thing.

'He had strength,' she said, dusting a group of lemonade bottles of various ages. 'Our Colin is going to be strong. He loved Colin.'

'Does he know?' asked Midgley.

'Yes. Only it hasn't hit him yet.'

Hoarse shouting and a rhythmic drumming on the floor indicated that his son was seeking solace in music.

'When it does hit him,' said his mother, picking at a spot of rust on a recently acquired Oxo tin, 'he is going to be genuinely heartbroken. There's always a gap. It was on *Woman's Hour*. Poor old Frank.'

'I've never understood,' said Midgley, 'why you call him Frank. He's my father.'

She looked at the 1953 Coronation mug, wondering if it was altogether too recent an artefact to have on display.

'He has a name. Frank is his name.'

It was not only the date, the Coronation mug was about the only object in the house Midgley had contributed to the decor, having been issued with it in 1953 when he was at primary school.

'I call him Dad,' said Midgley.

'He's not Dad, is he? Not my dad, I call him Frank because that's the name of a person. To me he is a person. That's why we get on.'

She was about to hide the mug behind a cast-iron money-box in the shape of a grinning black man then thought better of it. They had too many things. And there would be more coming from his dad. She cheered up slightly.

Her husband kissed her and opened the back door.

'It isn't though,' he said.

'It isn't what?'

'Why you get on. Treating him like a person.'

Seeing her stood there in her silly apron he felt sorry for her, and wished he had kept quiet.

'You get on,' he said (and because he was sorry for her tried to make it sound as if she was justified), 'you get on because you both despise me.'

'Listen.' She brought him away from the door and closed

it. Mrs Barnes next door, who had once described their marriage as uninhibited, was putting out a few opportune clothes. 'Your father is 74. He is dying. Considering the time you've been hanging about here he is possibly already dead yet you resent the fact that he and I were friends. I seem to have married someone very low down in the evolutionary chain. You might want one or two tissues.' And she darted at him and thrust them into his pocket.

Midgley opened the door again.

'It's just that when you and he were together I didn't exist.'

'I am married,' she shouted, 'to the cupboard under the sink.' A remark made more mysterious to Mrs Barnes by the sound of a passing ice-cream van playing the opening bars of the 'Blue Danube'.

'He is dying, Denis. Will you exist now? Will that satisfy you?' She was crying.

'I'll make it right, Joyce,' said Midgley. 'I'll be there when he goes. I'll hold his hand.'

He held hers, still in their Union Jack mittens. 'If I let him down now he'd stay with me the rest of my life. I did love him, Joyce.'

'I want him to stay with you the rest of your life. That's what I want. I think of his kindness. His unselfishness. His unflagging courtesy. The only incredible thing is that someone so truly saintly should have produced such a pill of a son.'

She took off Sylvia Plath and hung her behind the door. She had stopped crying.

'But I suppose that's your mother.'

'Shut up about my mother,' said Midgley.

His mother was a sore point. 'My mother is dead.'

'So is your father by now probably. Go!'

Midgley took her by the shoulders.

'Things will change then, you'll see. I'll change. I'll be a different person. I can . . . go. Live! Start!' He kissed her quickly and warmly and ran from the door down the little drive towards the van. His wife rushed to the door to catch him.

'Start?' she shouted. 'Start what? You're 39.'

'They had another do today,' Mrs Barnes told her husband that evening. 'It doesn't say much for a university education.'

Coming off the Leeds and Bradford Ring Road Midgley stopped at a zebra to let an old man cross. The old man held up a warning hand, and slowly moved across, glowering at the car. Midgley revved his engine and the old man stopped, glared and went on with seemingly deliberate slowness. Someone behind hooted. Midgley did not wait for the old man to reach the kerb but drove off with a jerk. Glancing in his mirror Midgley saw the old man slip and nearly fall.

At the hospital the first person he saw was Aunty Kitty, his father's sister. She said nothing, kissing him wordlessly, her eyes closed to indicate her grief lay temporarily beyond speech. The scene played she took his arm (something he disliked) and they followed the signs to Intensive Care.

'I thought you'd have been here a bit since,' said his Aunty. 'I've been here since two o'clock. You'll notice a big change.' They were going down a long featureless corridor. 'He's not like my brother. He's not the Frank I knew.' Visitors clustered at the doors of wards, waiting their turn to sit beside the beds of loved ones. Aunty Kitty favoured them with a brave smile. 'I don't dislike this colour scheme,' she said. 'I've always liked oatmeal. His doctor's black.'

Intensive Care had a waiting room to itself, presumably, Midgley thought, for the display of Intensive Grief, and there was a woman crying in the corner. 'Her hubby's on the critical list,' mouthed Aunty Kitty.

'Their eldest girl works for Johnson and Johnson. They'd just got back from Barbados. The nurse is white but she's not above eighteen.' The nurse came in. 'This is my nephew,' said Aunty Kitty. 'Mr Midgley's son. Your father's got a room to himself, love.'

'They all do,' said the nurse, 'at this stage.'

Midgley's father lay propped up against the pillows, staring straight ahead through the window at a blank yellow wall. His arms lay outside the coverlet, palms upward as if accepting his plight and awaiting some sort of deliverance. They had put him into some green hospital pyjamas, with half-length sleeves the functionalism of which seemed too modish to Midgley, who had only ever seen his father in bed in striped pyjamas, or sometimes his shirt. The garment was open and a monitor clung to his chest, and above the bed the television screen blipped steady and regular. Midgley watched it for a moment.

'Dad,' he said to himself.

'Dad. It's me, Denis.'

He put himself between the bed and the window so that if his father could see he would know he was there. He had read that stroke victims were never unconscious, just held in-

communicado. 'In the most solitary confinement,' the article had said, the writer himself a doctor and too much taken
with metaphor.

'It's all right, Dad.'

He took a chair and sat halfway down the bed, putting
his hand over his father's inert palm.

His father looked well in the face, which was ruddy and
worn, the skin of his neck giving way sharply to the white of
his body. The division between his known head and the unknown body had shocked Midgley when he had first seen it as
a child, when his Dad took him swimming at the local baths.
It was still the same. He had never sat in the sun all his life.

'I'm sorry, Dad,' said Midgley.

'Are you next of kin?' It was another nurse.

'Son.'

'Not too long then.'

'Is the doctor around?'

'Why? What do you want to know? There's nothing
wrong, is there? No complaints?'

'I want to know how he is.'

'He's very poorly. You can see.'

She looked down at her left breast and lifted a watch.

'Doctor'll be round in about an hour. He's very busy.'

'I wonder where he is,' said Aunty Kitty.

'She said he was busy.'

They were back in the waiting room.

Aunty Kitty looked at him with what he imagined she
imagined was a look of infinite sadness, mingled with pity
('Sorrow and love flow mingling down' came into his mind
from the hymn). 'Not the doctor, your dad, love. Behind that

stare he's somewhere, wandering. You know,' she said vaguely, 'in his mind. Where is he?'

She patted his hand.

'I don't suppose with having been to university you believe in an after-life. That's always the first casualty.'

For a while she read the small print on her pension book and Midgley thought about his childhood. Nurses came and went, leading their own lives and a man wiped plastic-covered mattresses in the corridor. Every time a nurse came near he made remarks like 'It's all right for some' or 'No rest for the wicked.' Once the matron glided silently by, majestic and serene on her electric trolley. 'They're a new departure,' said Aunty Kitty. 'I could do with one of those. I'll just pop and have another peep at your dad.'

'What does that look on his face mean?' she said when she came back. Midgley thought it meant he should have gone over to see him last Sunday. It meant that his dad had been right about him all along and now he was dying and whose fault was that? That was what it meant. 'This unit was opened by the Duchess of Kent,' said Aunty Kitty. 'They have a tip-top kidney department.'

The fascinations of medicine and royalty were equal in Aunty Kitty's mind and whenever possible she found a connection between the two. Had she been told she was dying but from the same disease as a member of the Royal Family she would have died happy.

'There's some waiting done in hospitals,' she said presently. 'Ninety per cent of it's waiting. Would you call this room oatmeal or cream?'

A young man came through, crying.

'His wife was in an accident,' Aunty Kitty explained. 'One of those head-on crashes. The car was a write-off. Did you come in your van?'

Midgley nodded.

'You'll be one of these two-car families, then? Would you say she was black?' A Thai nurse looked in briefly and went out again. 'You don't see that many of them. She's happen a refugee.'

Midgley looked at his watch. It was an hour since he had spoken to the nurse. He went in and stood at the desk but there was no one about. He stood at the door of his father's room. He had not moved, his unseeing eyes fixed on a window-cleaner, who with professional discretion carefully avoided their gaze.

'I always thought I'd be the first to go,' said Aunty Kitty, looking at an advertisement in *Country Life*. 'Fancy. Two swimming pools. I could do without two swimming pools. When you get to my age you just want somewhere you can get round nicely with the hoover. They've never got to the bottom of my complaint. They lowered a microscope down my throat but there was nothing. I wouldn't live in Portugal if they paid me. Minstrels' gallery, I shouldn't know what to do with a minstrels' gallery if I had one. Mr Penry-Jones wanted to put me on this machine the Duke of Gloucester inaugurated. This body-scan thing. Only there was such a long waiting-list apparently.'

A nurse came through.

'She's the one I was telling you about. I asked her if your dad was in a coma or just unconscious. She didn't know. They're taking them too young these days.'

'Aunty,' said Midgley.

'It isn't as if she was black. Black you don't expect them to know.'

'What was my dad like?'

Aunty Kitty thought for a moment.

'He never had a wrong word for anybody. He'd do anybody a good turn. Shovel their snow. Fetch their coal in. He was that type. He was a saint. You take after your mother more.'

'I feel I lack his sterling qualities,' said Midgley some time later. 'Grit. Patience. Virtues bred out of adversity.'

'You wouldn't think they'd have curtains in a hospital, would you?' said Aunty Kitty. 'You wouldn't think curtains would be hygienic. I'm not keen on purple anyway.'

'Deprivation for instance,' said Midgley.

'What?'

'I was never deprived. That way he deprived me. Do you understand?'

'I should have gone to secondary school,' she said. 'I left at thirteen, same as your dad.'

'I know I had it easier than he did,' said Midgley. 'But I was grateful. I didn't take it for granted.'

'You used to look bonny in your blazer.'

'It isn't particularly enjoyable, education.' Midgley had his head in his hands. 'I had what he wanted. Why should that be enjoyable?'

'Mark's got his bronze medal,' said Aunty Kitty. 'Did you not ought to be ringing round?'

'About the bronze medal?'

'About your dad.'

'I'll wait till I've seen the doctor.'

It was half-past six.

'They go on about these silicon chips, you'd think they'd get all these complaints licked first, somebody's got their priorities wrong. Then he's always been a right keen smoker has Frank. Now he's paying the price.'

Midgley fell asleep.

'Robert Donat had bronchitis,' said Aunty Kitty.

'Mr Midgley.' The doctor shook his shoulder.

'Denis,' said Aunt Kitty, 'it's doctor.'

He was a pale young Pakistani, and for a moment Midgley thought he had fallen asleep in class and was being woken by a pupil.

'Mr Midgley?' He was grave and precise, 26 at the most.

'Your father has had a stroke.' He looked at his clipboard. 'How severe it is hard to tell. When he was brought in he was suffering from hypothermia.'

Aunt Kitty gave a faint cry. It was a scourge that had been much in the news.

'He must have fallen and been lying there, two days at least.'

'I generally go over at weekends,' said Midgley.

'Pneumonia has set in. His heart is not strong. All things considered,' he looked at the clipboard again, 'we do not think he will last the night.'

As he went away he tucked the clipboard under his arm and Midgley saw there was nothing on it.

———

'Only three phones and two of them duff. You wouldn't credit it,' said a fat man. 'Say you were on standby for a transplant. It'd be just the same.' He jingled his coins and a young man in glasses on the working phone put his head outside the helmet.

'I've one or two calls to make,' he said cheerfully.

'Oh hell,' said the fat man.

'There's a phone outside physio. Try there,' said a passing nurse.

'I'll try there,' said the fat man.

Midgley sat on.

'Hello,' said the young man brightly. 'Dorothy? You're a grandma.' He looked at Midgley while he was talking, but without seeing him.

'A grandma,' he shouted. 'Yes!' There was a pause. 'Guess,' said the young man and listened. 'No,' he said. 'Girl. Seven and a half pounds. 5.35. Both doing well. I'm ringing everybody. Bye, Grandma.'

Midgley half rose as the young man put the receiver back, but sat back as he consulted a bit of paper then picked it up again and dialled.

'Hello, Neil. Hi. You're an uncle . . . You're an uncle. Today. Just now. 5.35. Well, guess.' He waited. 'No. Girl. No. I'm over the moon. So you can tell Christine she's an aunty. Yes, a little cousin for Josephine. How's it feel to be an uncle? . . . Bye.'

Midgley got up and stood waiting. The young man took another coin and dialled again. It was a way of breaking news that could be adapted for exits as well as entrances, thought Midgley.

'Hello, Margaret. You're a widow. A widow . . . This afternoon. Half-past two . . . How's it feel to be bereaved?'

'Betty,' said the young man. 'Congratulations.

'You're an aunty. Aunty Betty. I won't ask you to guess,' he went on hurriedly. 'It's a girl. Susan's over the moon. And I am.'

With each call his enthusiasm had definitely decreased. Midgley reflected that this baby was well on the way to being a bore and it was only a couple of hours old.

'I'm just telephoning with the glad tidings. Bye, Aunty.'

The proud father put a new pile of coins on the box and Midgley was moved to intervene.

'Could I just make one call?'

'Won't it wait,' said the young man. 'I was here first. I'm a father.'

'I'm a son,' said Midgley. 'My father's dying.'

'There's no need to take that tone,' said the young man, stepping out of the helmet. 'You should have spoken up. There's a phone outside physio.'

Midgley listened to the phone ringing along the passage at his father's brother's house.

'Uncle Ernest? It's Denis. Dad's been taken poorly.'

'You mean Frank?' said his uncle.

'Yes. Dad. He's had a stroke,' said Midgley. 'And a fall. And now he's got pneumonia.' Somehow he felt he ought to have selected two out of three, not laid everything on the line first go off.

'Oh dear, oh dear, oh dear,' said his uncle. 'Our Frank.'

'Can you ring round and tell anybody who might want to come. The doctor says he won't last the night.'

'From here? Me ring?'

It started pipping.

'Yes. I'm in a box. There are people waiting.'

'You never know,' said the young man. 'They can work miracles nowadays.'

'This is what I'd call an industrial lift,' said Uncle Ernest, tapping the wall with his strong boot. 'It's not an ordinary passenger lift, this. It's as big as our sitting room.'

It stopped and a porter slid a trolley in beside Midgley. A woman looked up at him and smiled faintly.

'Is it working?' said the porter. The little head closed its eyes.

'We've just had a nice jab and now we're going for a ta ta.'

Behind a glass panel Midgley watched the concrete floors pass.

'It's very solidly constructed,' said Uncle Ernest, looking at the floor. 'These are overlapping steel plates. We can still do it when we try.'

'Let the dog see the rabbit,' said the porter as the lift stopped.

'This is six,' said Midgley.

'Every floor looks the same to me,' said his uncle.

'Did you ring our Hartley?' Hartley was Uncle Ernest's son and a chartered accountant.

'He's coming as soon as he can get away.'

'Was he tied up?'

He had been.

'Secretary was it? Was he in a meeting? I'd like to know what they are, these meetings he's always in, that he can't speak to his father. "Excuse me, I have to speak to my father." That's no disgrace, is it? "I won't be a moment, my dad's on the line." Who's going to take offence at that? Who are they, in these meetings? Don't they have fathers? I thought fathers were universal. Instead of which I have to make an appointment to see my own son. Sons, fathers, you shouldn't need appointments. You should get straight through. You weren't like that with your dad. Frank thought the world of you.'

They were going down the long corridor again.

'I came on the diesel,' said Uncle Ernest. He was lame in one leg.

'I go all over. I went to York last week. Saw the railway museum. There's stock in there I drove. Museum in my own lifetime. I'll tell you one thing.'

They stopped.

'What,' said Midgley.

'I wouldn't like to have to polish this floor.'

They resumed.

'You still schoolteaching?'

Midgley nodded.

'Pleased your dad, did that. Though it won't be much of a salary. You'd have been better off doing something in our Hartley's line. He's up there in the £30,000 bracket now. She was talking about a swimming pool.'

They stopped at the entrance to Intensive Care while his uncle stood, one arm stretched out to the wall, taking the weight off his leg.

'Is your Aunty Kitty here?'

'Yes.'

'I thought she would be. Where no vultures fly.'

Aunty Kitty got up and did her 'I am too upset to speak' act. 'Hello, Kitty,' said Ernest.

'I always thought I should be the first, Ernest.'

'Well you still might be. He's not dead yet.'

'Go in, Ernest.' She dabbed her nose. 'Go in.'

Uncle Ernest stood by his brother's bed. Then he sat down.

'This is summat fresh for you, Frank,' he said. 'You were always such a bouncer.' He stood up and leaned over the bed to look closer at the bleeps on the scanner. They were bouncing merrily. A nurse looked in.

'You're not to touch that.'

'I was just interested.'

'He's very ill.'

She paused for a moment, came further into the room and looked at the scanner. She looked at Uncle Ernest (though not, he noticed, at Frank) and went out.

'It's all mechanised now,' he said.

There was no sound in the room. The brothers had never had much to say to each other at the best of times. Without there being any animosity, they felt easier in the presence of a third party; alone they embarrassed each other. It was still the case, even though one of them was unconscious, and Uncle Ernest got up, thankful to be able to go.

'Ta-ra then, butt,' he said.

And waited.

He wanted to pat his brother's hand.

'I went to York last week,' he said. 'It hasn't changed much. They haven't spoiled it like they have Leeds. Though there's one of these precinct things. It's the first time I've been since we were lads. We went over on our bikes once.' Instead of touching his brother's hand he jogged his foot in farewell, just as the nurse was coming in.

'He's very ill,' she said, smoothing the coverlet over his brother's feet. 'And this is delicate equipment.'

'I went in,' she said in the canteen later, 'and there was one of them pulling a patient's leg about. He had hold of his foot. It's an uphill battle.'

Uncle Ernest's son Hartley came with his wife Jean and their children, Mark (14) and Elizabeth (10). Hartley hated hospitals, hence his demand for full family back-up. He was actually surprised that Mark had condescended to come: a big 14, Mark had long since passed beyond parental control and only appeared with the family on state occasions. The truth was that Miss Pollock, who took him for Religious Knowledge and who was known to be fucking at least one of the sixth form, had pointed out only last week how rare were the opportunities these days of seeing a dead person, and thus of acquiring a real perspective on the human condition. Mark was hoping this visit might gain him some status in the eyes of Miss Pollock. Sensitive to the realities of birth and death, he hoped to be the next candidate for 'bringing out'.

They were all going up in the lift.

'Think on,' said Hartley. 'It's quite likely your grandad'll be here. I don't want you asking for all sorts in front of him.'

'No,' said his wife. 'We don't want him saying you're spoiled.'

'Though you are spoiled,' said Hartley.

'Whose fault is that?' said Jean.

The steel doors folded back to reveal Denis saying goodbye to Uncle Ernest.

'Now then, Dad,' said Hartley. 'Hello, Denis. This is a bad do.'

Jean kissed the old man.

'Give your grandad a kiss, Elizabeth.'

The child did so.

'Come on, Mark.'

'I don't kiss now,' said the boy.

'You kiss your grandad,' said Hartley and the boy did so and a nurse, passing, looked.

'How is he?' said Hartley.

'Dying,' said his father. 'Sinking fast.'

'Oh dear, oh dear, oh dear,' said Hartley, who had hoped it would be all over by now.

'And how've you been keeping?' said Jean, brightly.

'Champion,' said Uncle Ernest. 'Is that one of them new watches?' He took Mark's wrist.

'He had to save up for it,' said Jean. 'You had to save up for it, didn't you, Mark?'

Mark nodded.

'He didn't,' said the little girl.

'I never had a watch till I was 21,' said the old man. 'Of course, they're 21 at 18 now, aren't they?'

Denis pressed the button for the lift.

'We'd better get along to the ward if he's that critical,' said Jean.

'I've had the receiver in my hand to give you a ring once or twice,' said Hartley as they waited for the lift, 'then a client's come in.'

'I was thinking of going to Barnard Castle next week,' said Ernest.

'Whatever for?' said Jean, kissing him goodbye.

'I've never been.' He shook Denis's hand. The lift doors closed. Hartley and his family walked ahead of Midgley down the long corridor.

'I'll give you such a clatter when I get you home, young lady,' Jean was saying. 'He did save up.'

'Only a week,' said the child.

'When we get there,' said Hartley, 'we want to go in in twos. All together would be too much of a strain.'

'What's he doing going to Barnard Castle?' said Jean. 'He can't be short of money taking himself off to Barnard Castle.'

Midgley caught them up.

'You'd no need all to come,' he said. 'I wouldn't let Joyce bring ours.'

'They wanted to come,' said Jean. 'Our Mark did especially, didn't you Mark?'

'It's more handy for us, anyway,' said Hartley. 'What did we do before the M62?'

Mark was disappointed. The old man was quite plainly breathing. He could quite easily have been asleep. He wasn't even white.

'He's not my uncle, is he, Dad?'

'He's my uncle. He's your great-uncle.'

Hartley was looking at the screen.

'You see this screen, Mark? It's monitoring his heartbeats.'

Mark didn't look, but said wearily, 'I know, Dad.'

'I was only telling you.'

Hartley touched the screen where the beep was flickering.

'You want to learn, don't you?' his father said as they came out.

'Dad.' The boy stopped. 'We made one of those at school.'

Jean now led little Elizabeth in. ('Bless her,' said Aunty Kitty.)

They stood hand in hand by the bedside, and Jean bent down and kissed him.

'Do you want me to kiss him?' said the child.

'No. I don't think so, love,' and she rubbed her lips with her hanky where they had touched him.

'Are you crying, Mam?' said the child.

'Yes.'

The little girl looked up at her.

'There aren't any tears.'

'You can cry without tears,' said her mother, looking at the monitor. 'You can cry more without tears.'

'I can't,' said the child. 'How do you do it, Mam?'

'It comes when you're grown up.'

'I want to be able to do it now.'

'Listen, I'll give you such a smack in a minute,' said her mother. 'He's dying.'

Elizabeth began to cry.

'There, love.' Her mother hugged her. 'He doesn't feel it.'

'I'm not crying because of him,' said the child. 'I'm crying because of you.'

'I wouldn't have another Cortina,' said Hartley. 'I used to swear by Cortinas. No longer.'

Midgley was watching an Indian man and his son sat in the corner. The father's face ran with tears as he hugged the child to him so that he seemed in danger of smothering the boy.

'You still got the VW?'

Midgley nodded.

'I think I might go in for a Peugeot,' said Hartley. 'A 604. Buy British.' There was a pause, and he added:

'He was a nice old chap.'

Jean and Elizabeth returned and Mark, who had been in the corridor, came in to ask how long they were stopping.

Hartley looked at Jean.

'I think we ought to wait just a bit, don't you, darling?'

'Oh yes,' said Jean. 'Just in case.'

Aunty Kitty came in. 'I've just had one coffee and a wagon wheel and it was 45p. And it's all supposed to be voluntary.'

'There isn't a disco, is there?' said Mark.

'Disco?' said Jean. 'Disco? This is a hospital.'

'Well. Leisure facilities. Facilities for visitors. Killing time.'

'Listen,' Jean hissed. 'Your Uncle Denis's father is dying and you talk about discos.'

'It's all right,' said Midgley.

'Here, go get yourself a coffee,' said Hartley, giving him a pound. Aunty Kitty looked away.

Hartley and his family were going. They were congregated outside the lift.

'You'll wait, I expect,' said Hartley.

'Oh yes,' said Midgley, 'I want to be here.'

'You want to make it plain at this stage you don't want him resuscitating.'

'That's if he doesn't want him resuscitating,' said Jean. 'You don't know.'

'I wouldn't want my dad resuscitating,' said Hartley.

'Denis might, mightn't you, Denis?'

'No,' said Midgley.

'You often don't get the choice,' said Hartley. 'They'll resuscitate anybody given half a chance. Shove them on these life-support machines. It's all to do with cost-effectiveness. They invest in this expensive equipment then they feel they have to use it.' He pumped the lift button. 'My guess is that it'll be at four in the morning, the crucial time. That's when life's at its lowest ebb, the early hours.'

'Miracles do happen, of course,' said Jean. 'I was reading about these out-of-body experiences. Have you read about them, Denis? It's where very sick people float in the air above their own bodies. Personally,' Jean kissed Midgley, 'I think it won't be long before science will be coming round to an after-life. Bye bye. I wish it had been on a happier occasion.'

Midgley went down the long corridor.

'Money's no good,' said Aunty Kitty. 'Look at President Kennedy. They've been a tragic family.'

The Indians slept, the little son laid with his head in the father's lap.

An orderly came in and tidied the magazines, emptied the waste-bin and took away a vase of flowers.

'Oxygen,' he said as he went out.

'The Collingwoods got back from Corfu,' said Aunty Kitty. 'They said they enjoyed it but they wouldn't go a second time.'

It was after ten and Midgley had assumed she was going to stay the night when she suddenly got up.

'If I go now I can get the twenty-to,' she said. 'I'll just get back before they're turning out. I never go upstairs. It's just asking for it.'

'I'll walk down with you,' said Midgley.

She tiptoed elaborately past the sleeping immigrants, favouring them with a benevolent smile.

'They've got feelings the same as us,' she whispered. 'They're fond of their families. More so, probably.' They came out into the corridor. 'But then they're less advanced than we are.'

He phoned Joyce.

She and Colin were watching a programme about dolphins that had been introduced by the Duke of Edinburgh. Her mother was asleep with her mouth open.

'What're you doing?' asked Midgley.

'Nothing. Colin's watching a programme about dolphins. How is he?'

Midgley told her.

'I've got to stay,' he finished.

'Why? You've done all that's necessary. Nobody's going to blame you.'

Midgley saw that somebody had written on the wall 'Pray for me.' A wag had added 'OK.'

'I must be here when he goes,' said Midgley. 'You can understand that.'

'I understand you,' she said. 'It's not love. It's not affection.' Colin looked up. 'It's yourself.'

She put the phone down.

'Dad?' said Colin.

She turned the television off. 'He's hanging on.'

'Who?'

'Your grandad.' She got up. 'Wake up Mother. Time for bed.'

Midgley went back and sat with his father. While he had been out the night nurse had come on. She was a plump girl, dark, less pert than the others, and, he thought, more human. Actually she was just dirty. The hair wasn't gathered properly under her cap and there was a ladder in her stocking. She straightened the bedclothes, bending over the inert form so that her behind was inches from Midgley's face. Midgley decided it wasn't deliberate.

'Am I in the way?' he asked.

'No,' she said. 'Why? Stop there.'

She looked at the television monitor for a minute or two, counting the jumps with her watch. Then she smiled

and went out. Five minutes later she was back with a cup
of tea.

'No sugar,' said Midgley.

'May I?' she said and put both lumps in her mouth.

'Slack tonight,' she said. 'Still it just needs one drunken
driver.'

Midgley closed his eyes.

'I thought you were going to be a bit of company,' she said.
'You're tired out.' She fetched a pillow and they went out into
the waiting room. The Indians had gone.

'Lie down,' she said. 'I'll wake you if anything happens.'

Around five an alarm went off, and there were two deaths
in quick succession. Midgley slept on. At eight he woke.

'You can't lie down,' said a voice. 'You're not supposed to
lie down.' It was a clean, fresh nurse.

Two women he had not seen before sat watching him.

'The nurse said she'd wake me up.'

'What nurse?'

'If anything happened to my father.'

'Whose is that pillow?'

'Midgley. Mr Midgley.'

'It's a hospital pillow.' She took it, and went back inside
to her desk.

'Midgley.' Her finger ran down the list. 'No change. But
don't lie down. It's not fair on other people.'

Midgley went and looked at his father. No change was
right. He felt old and dirty. He had not shaved and there was
a cold sore starting on his lip. But with his father there
was no change. Still clean. Still pink. Still breathing. The dot
skipped on. He walked out to the car park where he had left

his van and wondered if he dared risk going out to buy a razor.

He went back in search of the doctor.

He cut across the visitors' car park, empty now except for his van, and took a path round the outside of the hospital that he thought would take him round to the entrance. The buildings were long and low and set in the hillside. They were done in identical units, every ward the same. He was passing a ward that seemed just like his father's except where his father should have been a woman was just putting her breast to a baby's mouth. A nurse came to the window and stared at him. He looked away hurriedly and walked on, but not so quickly as to leave her with the impression he had been watching. She was still staring at him as he turned the corner. He experienced a feeling of relief if not quite homecoming when he saw he was now outside Intensive Care. He picked out his father's room, saw the carnations on the windowsill and the head and shoulders of a nurse. She was obviously looking at the bed. She moved back towards the window to make room for someone else. Midgley stood on tiptoe to try and see what was happening. He thought there was someone else there in a white coat. The room was full of people.

Midgley ran round the unit trying to find a way in. There was a door at the end of the building with an empty corridor beyond. It was locked. He ran up to the path again, then cut down across the bank through some young trees to try another door. A man on the telephone watched him sliding down then put one phone down and picked up another. Midgley ran on and suddenly was in a muddy flower bed among bushes and evergreens. It was the garden around the

entrance to the Reception Area. Upstairs he ran past the startled nurse at the desk and into his father's room. Nobody
spoke. There was an atmosphere of reverence.

'Is he dead?' said Midgley. 'Has he gone?' He was pant-
ing. An older woman in blue turned round. 'Dead? Certainly
not. I am the matron. And look at your shoes.'

Behind the matron Midgley caught a glimpse of his
father. As a nurse bustled him out Midgley struggled to
look back. He was sure his father was smiling.

'I've just been to spend a penny,' said Aunty Kitty. 'When
you consider it's a hospital the toilets are nothing to write
home about. Look at your shoes.'

She was beginning to settle in, had brought a flask,
sandwiches, knitting.

'I know Frank,' she said, looking at *Country Life*. 'He'll
make a fight of it. I wouldn't thank you for a place in Bermuda.'

Midgley went to the gents to have a wash. He got some
toilet paper and stood by the basins wiping the mud off his
boots. He was stood with the muddy paper in his hands when
an orderly came in, looked at the paper then looked at him
incredulously, shook his head and went into a cubicle saying:
'The fucking public. The fucking dirty bastard public.'

Midgley went down to ring his Uncle Ernest on the phone
outside physio. A youngish woman was just dialling.

'Cyril. It's . . .' She held the mouthpiece away from her
mouth and the earpiece from her ear. 'It's Vi. Vi. I am speaking into it. Mum's had her op. No. She's had it. Had it this
morning first thing. She's not come round yet, but I spoke to
the sister and apparently she's fine. FINE. And the sister
says . . .' She dropped her voice. 'It wasn't what we thought.

It wasn't what we thought. No. So there's no need to worry.' She ran her finger over the acoustic headboard behind the phone, fingering the holes. 'No. Completely clear. Well I think it's good news, don't you? The sister said the surgeon is the best. Mr Caldecott. People pay thousands to have him. Anyway I'm so relieved. Aren't you? Yes. Bye.'

As Midgley took the phone she took out her handkerchief and rubbed it over her lips, and safely outside the hospital, her ear.

Uncle Ernest had said on the phone that if this was going to go on he wasn't sure he could run to the fares, but he turned up in the late afternoon along with Hartley.

He went and sat with his brother for a bit, got down and looked under the bed and figured out how the mechanism worked that lifted and lowered it and finally stood up and said, 'Gillo, Frank,' which was what he used to say when they went out cycling between the wars. It meant 'hurry up'.

'It's Frank all over,' said Aunty Kitty, 'going down fighting. He loved life.'

There were a couple of newcomers in the waiting room, an oldish couple.

'It's their eldest daughter,' whispered Aunty Kitty. 'She was just choosing some new curtains in Schofields. Collapsed. Suspected brain haemorrhage. Their other son's a vet.'

They trailed down the long corridor to the lift.

'It's a wonder to me,' said Uncle Ernest, 'how your Aunty Kitty's managed to escape strangulation all these years. Was he coloured, this doctor?'

'Which?' said Midgley.

'That said he was on his last legs.'

Midgley reluctantly admitted he was.

'That explains it,' said the old railwayman.

'Dad,' said Hartley.

'What does that mean, "Dad"?' said his father.

'It means I'm vice-chairman of the community relations council. It means we've got one in the office and he's a tip-top accountant. It means we all have to live with one another in this world.' He pumped the button of the lift.

'I'll not come again,' said Uncle Ernest. 'It gets morbid.'

'We've just got to play it by ear,' said Hartley.

'You won't have this performance with me,' said the old man. 'Come once and have done.'

'Shall I drop you?' said Hartley as the doors opened.

'I don't want you to go out of your way.'

'No, but shall I drop you?'

'Press G,' said Uncle Ernest.

The lift doors closed.

Midgley was sitting with his father when the plump night nurse came on.

'I wondered if you'd be on tonight.' He read her tab. 'Nurse Lightfoot.'

'Waiting for me, were you? No change.' She took a tissue and wiped the old man's mouth. 'He doesn't want to leave us, does he?' She picked up the vase of carnations from the windowsill. 'Oxygen,' she said and took them outside.

Later, when she had made him a cup of tea and Aunty Kitty

had gone home for the second night, he was sitting at the bedside but got up when she started to give his father a bed bath.

'You're like one another.'

He stared out of the window, even moved to avoid seeing the reflection.

'No,' he said.

'You are. It's a compliment. He has a nice face.' She sponged under his arms.

'What are you?' she said.

'How do you mean?' He turned just as she had folded back the sheets and was sponging between his legs. Quickly he looked out of the window again.

'What do you do?'

'Teacher. I'm a teacher.' He wanted to go and sit in the waiting room.

'What was he?'

'Plumber.'

'He's got lovely hands. Real ladies' hands.'

And it was true. She had finished and the soft white hands of his father lay over the sheet.

'That happens in hospitals. People's hands change.' She held his father's hand. Midgley wondered if he could ask her to hold his. Probably. She looked even more of a mess than the night before.

'Is there anything you want to ask?'

'Yes,' said Midgley.

'If there is, doctor'll be round in a bit.'

It was a different doctor. Not Indian. Fair, curly-haired and aged not much more than fourteen.

'His condition certainly hasn't deteriorated,' the child said. 'On the other hand,' he glanced boyishly at the chart, 'it can't be said to have improved.'

Midgley wondered if he had ever had his ears pierced.

'I don't know that there's any special point in waiting. You've done your duty.' He gave him a winning smile and had Midgley been standing closer would probably have put his hand on his arm as he had been taught to do.

'After all,' he was almost conspiratorial, 'he doesn't know you're here.'

'I don't think he's dying,' said Midgley.

'Living, dying,' said the boy and shrugged. The words meant the same thing.

'You do want your father to live?' He turned towards the nurse and pulled a little face.

'I was told he wasn't going to last long. I live in Hull.'

'Our task is to make them last as long as possible.' The pretty boy looked at his watch. 'We've no obligation to get them off on time.'

'Some of them seem to think we're British Rail,' the doctor remarked to a nurse in the small hours when they were having a smoke after sexual intercourse.

'I don't like 15-year-old doctors, that's all,' said Midgley. 'I'm old enough to be his father. Does nobody else wait? Does nobody else feel they have to be here?'

'Why not go sleep in your van? I can give you a pillow and things.' She was eating a toffee. 'I'll send somebody down to the car park if anything happens.'

'What do you do all day?' asked Midgley.

'Sleep.' She was picking a bit of toffee from her tooth. 'I generally surface around three.'

'Maybe we could have a coffee. If he's unchanged.'

'OK.'

She smiled. He had forgotten how easy it was.

'I'll just have another squint at my dad.'

He came back. 'Come and look. I think he's moved.'

She ran ahead of him into the room. The old man lay back on the pillows, a shaded light by the bed.

'You had me worried for a moment,' she said. 'It's all right.'

'No. His face has changed.'

She switched on the lamp over the bed, the light so sudden and bright that that alone might have made the old man flinch. But nothing moved.

'It's just that he seemed to be smiling.'

'You're tired,' she said, put her hand against his face and switched out the light.

Midgley switched it on again.

'If you look long enough at him you'll see a smile.'

'If you look long enough,' she said, walking out of the room, 'you'll see anything you want.'

Midgley stood for a moment in the darkened room, wishing he had kissed her when he'd had the chance. He went out to look for her but there had been a pileup on the M62 and all hell was about to break loose.

'What do you do all day?' said his wife on the phone. 'Sit in the waiting room. Sit in his room. Walk round the hospital.

'Don't they mind?'

'Not if they're going to die.'

'Is he, though?' said his wife, watching her mother who had taken up her station on the chair by the door, holding her bag on her knees, preparatory to going to bed. 'It seems a long time.' The old lady was falling asleep. Once she had slipped right off that chair and cracked her head on the sideboard. That had been a hospital do.

'I can't talk. Mum's waiting to go up. She's crying out for a bath. I'm just going to have to steel myself.' The handbag slipped to the floor.

'I need a bath,' said Midgley.

'Go over to your dad's,' said his wife. 'Mum's falling over. Bye.'

'What am I doing sat on this seat?' said her mother, as she got her up. 'I never sit on this seat. I don't think I've ever sat on this seat before.'

In the morning Midgley was woken by Nurse Lightfoot banging on the steamed-up window of the van. It was seven o'clock.

'I'm just going off,' she was mouthing through the glass.

He wound down the window.

'I'm just coming off. Isn't it a grand morning? I'm going to have a big fried breakfast then go to bed. I'll see you at teatime. You look terrible.'

Midgley looked at himself in the driving mirror, then started up the van and drove after her, hooting.

'You're not supposed to hoot,' she said. 'It's a hospital.'

'I forgot to ask you. How's my dad?'

'No change.' She waved and ran down a grass bank to-wards the nurses' flats. 'No change.'

His dad lived where he had lived once, at the end of a ter-race of redbrick back-to-back houses. It was an end house, as his mother had always been careful to point out. It gave them one more window, which was nice, only kids used the end wall to play football against, which wasn't. His dad used to heave himself up from the fireside and go out to them, night after night. He let himself in with the key he had had since he was 14. 'You're 21 now,' his mother had said.

The house was neat and clean and cold. He looked for some sign of interrupted activity, even a chair out of place, some clue as to what his father had been doing when the blow fell. But there was nothing. He had a home help. She had probably tidied up. He put the kettle on, before having a shave. He knew where everything was. His dad's razor on the shelf above the sink, a shaving brush worn down to a stub and a half-used packet of Seven O'Clock blades. He scrubbed away the caked rust from the razor ('Your dad doesn't care,' said his mother) and put in a new blade. He had never gone in for shaving soap. Puritan soap they always bought, green Puritan soap. Then having shaved he took his shirt off to wash in the same sequence he had seen his father follow every night when he came in from work. Then, thinking of the coming afternoon, he did something he had never seen his father do, take off his trousers and his pants to wash his cock. He smelled his shirt. It stank. Naked, white and shiv-ering he went through the neat sitting room and up the nar-row stairs and stood on the cold lino of his parents' bedroom looking at himself in the dressing-table mirror. On top of the dressing-table, stood on little lace mats, was a toilet set. A round glass jar for a powder-puff, a pin tray, a cut-glass dish with a small pinnacle in the middle, for rings, and a celluloid-backed mirror and hairbrush. Items that had never had a practical use, but which had lain there in their appointed place for forty years.

He opened the dressing-table drawer, and found a new shirt still in its packet. They had given it to his father as a Christmas present two years before. He put it on, carefully extracting all the pins and putting them in the cut-glass dish. He looked for pants and found a pair that were old, baggy and gone a bit yellow. Some socks. Nothing quite fitted. He was smaller than his father. These days it was generally the other way round. He went downstairs, through into the scullery to polish his shoes. He remembered the brushes, the little brush to put the polish on which as a child he had always thought of as bad, the big noble brush that brought out the shine. He stood on the hearth rug and saw himself in the mirror, ready as if for a funeral, and sat down on the settee about to weep when he realised it was not his father's funeral he was imagining but his own. On the end of the tiled mantelpiece of which his mother had been so proud when they had had it put in in 1953 (a crime getting rid of that beautiful range, Joyce always said) was his dad's pipe. It was still half full of charred tobacco. He put it back but rolling over it fell onto the hearth. He stooped to pick it up and was his father suddenly, bending down, falling and lying there two days with the pipe under his hand. He dashed out of the house and drove wildly back to the hospital.

'No change,' said the nurse wearily (they were beginning

to think he was mad). But if there was no change at least the old man didn't seem to be smiling.

'I'm wearing your shirt, Dad,' Midgley said. 'The one we gave you for Christmas. I hope that's all right. It doesn't really suit me, but I think that's why Joyce bought it. She said it didn't suit me but it would suit you.'

A nurse came in.

'They tell you to talk,' said Midgley. 'I read it in an article in the *Reader's Digest*,' (and as if this gave it added force), 'it was in the waiting room.'

The nurse sniffed. 'They say the same thing about plants,' she said, putting the carnations back on the windowsill. 'I think it's got past that stage.'

Midgley was sitting on the divan bed in Nurse Lightfoot's room in the nurses' quarters. The rooms were light and modern like the hospital. She was sitting by the electric fire with one bar on. There was a Snoopy poster on the wall.

'People are funny about nurses,' she said. 'Men.' She took a bite of her bun. They were muesli buns. 'You say you're a nurse and their whole attitude changes. Do you know what I mean?'

'No,' lied Midgley.

'I notice it at parties particularly. They ask you what you do, you say you're a nurse and next minute they've got you on the floor. Perfectly ordinary people turn into wild beasts.' She switched another bar on.

'I've given up saying I'm a nurse for that reason.'

'What do you say you are?' asked Midgley. He wondered

whether he would be better placed if he went over to the fire or he got her to come over to the bed.

'I say I'm a sales representative. I don't mean you,' she said. 'You're obviously not like that. Course you've got other things on your mind at the moment.'

'Like what?'

'Your dad.'

'Oh yes.'

The duty nurse had been instructed to ring if there was any sign of a crisis.

'He is lovely,' she said, through mouthfuls of bun. 'I do understand the way you feel about him.'

'Do you?' said Midgley. 'That's nice.'

'Old people have their own particular attraction. He's almost sexy.'

Midgley stood up suddenly.

She picked something out of her mouth.

'Was your cake gritty?'

'No,' said Midgley, sitting down again.

'Mine was. Mine was a bit gritty.'

'It was probably meant to be gritty,' said Midgley, looking at his watch.

'No. It was more gritty than that.'

'What would you say,' asked Midgley, as he carefully examined a small stain on the bedcover, 'what would you say if I asked you to go to bed.'

'Now?' she asked, extracting another piece of grit or grain.

'If you like.' He made it sound as if she had made the suggestion.

'I can't now.' She gathered up the cups and plates.

'Why not? You're not on till seven.'

'It's Wednesday. I'm on early turn.' She wondered if he was going to turn into a wild beast.

'Tomorrow then?'

'Tomorrow would be better. Though of course it all depends.'

'What on?'

She was shocked.

'Your father. He may not be here tomorrow.'

'That's true,' said Midgley, getting up. He kissed her fairly formally.

'Anyway,' she smiled. 'Fingers crossed.'

Midgley sat by his father's bed and watched the dot skipping on the screen.

'Hold on, Dad,' he muttered. 'Hold on.'

There was no change.

Before going down to sleep in the van he telephoned home. It was his son who answered. Joyce was upstairs with her mother.

'Could you ask her to come to the phone, please,' said Midgley. The 'please' was somehow insulting. He heard brief shouting.

'She can't,' said Colin. 'Gran's in the bath. Mum can't leave her. What do you want?'

'You go up and watch her while I speak to your Mum.'

'Dad.' The boy's voice was slow with weary outrage. 'Dad. She's in the bath. She's no clothes on. I don't want to see her.'

He heard more distant shouting.

'Mum says if she can get a granny-sitter she may come over to see Grandad.'

'Colin.' Midgley was suddenly urgent. 'Colin. Are you still there?'

'Sure.' (Midgley hated that.)

'Tell her not to do that. Do you hear? Tell her there's no need to come over. Go on, tell her.'

'I'll tell her when she comes down.'

'No,' said Midgley. 'Now. I know you. Go up and tell her now.'

The phone was put down and he could hear Colin bellowing up the stairs. He came back.

'I told her. Is that all?'

'No,' said Midgley. 'Haven't you forgotten something? How's Grandad? Haven't you forgotten that? Well it's nice of you to ask, Colin. He's about the same, Colin, thank you.'

'How was your grandad?' said Joyce, coming downstairs with a wet towel and a bundle of her mother's underclothes.

'About the same,' said Colin.

'And your dad?'

'No change.'

That night Midgley dreamed it was morning when the door opened and his father got into the van.

'I didn't know you drove, Dad,' he said as they were going into town. 'When did you learn?'

'Just before I died.'

His mother, as a girl, met them outside the Town Hall.

'What a spanking van, Frank,' she said. 'Move up, Denis, let me sit next to your dad.'

The three of them sat in a row until he saw her hand was on his father's leg, when suddenly he was in a field alone with his mother.

'What a grand field,' she said. 'It's spotless.'

He was a little boy and she was in a white frock, and some terrible threat had just been lifted. Then he looked behind him and saw something much worse. On the edge of the field, ready to engulf them, was an enormous slag heap, glinting black and shiny in the sun. His mother hadn't seen it and chattered on how lovely this field was and slipping nearer came this terrible hill. Someone ran down the slope, waving his arms, a figure big and filthy, a miner, a coalman. He slid down beside them.

'Oh,' she said placidly, 'here's your father,' and he sat down beside her, coal and muck all over her white frock.

Then they were walking through Leeds Market. It was Sunday and the stalls were empty and shuttered. It was also a church and they walked up through the market to the choir screen. It was in the form of a board announcing Arrivals and Departures, slips of board clicking over with names on them, only instead of Arrivals and Departures it was headed Births and Deaths. Midgley wandered off while his parents sat looking at the board. Then his mam got up and kissed his dad, and went backwards through the screen just before the gates were drawn across. Midgley tried to run down the church and couldn't. He was shouting 'Mam. Mam.' Eventually he got to the gates and started shaking them, but she had gone. He turned to look at his father who shook his head slowly and turned away. Midgley went on rattling the gates then someone was shaking the van. It was Nurse Lightfoot waking him up. 'You can call me Valery,' she chanted as she ran off to her big breakfast.

Later that morning Midgley went in to see his father to find a smartish middle-aged woman sat by the bed. She was holding his father's hand.

'Is it Denis?' she said without getting up.

'Yes.'

'I'm Alice Dugdale. Did he tell you about me?'

'No.'

'He wouldn't, being him. He's an old bugger. Aren't you?'

She shook the inert hand. She was in her fifties, Midgley decided, very confident and done up to the nines. His mother would have called her common. She looked like the wife of a prosperous licensee.

'He told me about you,' she said. 'He never stopped telling me about you. It's a sad sight.'

The nurse had said his father was a bit better this morning.

'His condition's stabilised,' said Midgley.

'Yes, she said that to me, the little slut. What does she know?' She looked at him. 'You're a bit scruffy.' She stood up and smoothed down her skirt. 'I've come from Southport.' She took the carnations from the vase and put them in the waste-bin. 'A depressing flower, carnations,' she said. 'I prefer freesias. I'm a widow,' she said. 'A rich widow. Shall we have a meander round? No sense in stopping here.' She kissed his father on the forehead. 'His lordship's not got much to contribute. Bye bye chick.'

She swept through the waiting room with Midgley in her wake. Aunty Kitty open-mouthed got up and went out to watch them going down the corridor.

'That'll be your Aunty Kitty, I take it.' She said it loudly enough for her to hear.

'It is, yes,' said Denis, glancing back and smiling weakly. 'Do you know her?'

'No, thank God. Though she probably knows me.'

They found a machine and had some coffee. She took a silver flask from her bag.

'Do you want some of this in it?'

'No thanks,' said Midgley.

'I'd better,' she said. 'I've driven from Southport. I wanted to marry your dad only he said no. I had too much money. My husband left me very nicely placed. He was a leading light in the soft furnishing trade. Frank would have felt beholden, you see. That was your dad all over. Still you know what he was like.'

Midgley was no longer sure he did.

'How do you mean?' he said.

'He always had to be the one, did Frank. The one who did the good turns, the one who paid out, the one who sacrificed. You couldn't do anything for him. I had all this money and he wouldn't even let me take him to Scarborough. We used to go sit in Roundhay Park. Roundhay Park!'

A woman went by, learning to use crutches.

'We could have been in Tenerife.'

Midgley was glad to have at least this aspect of his father's character confirmed.

'I didn't want to let him down,' said Midgley. 'That's why I've been waiting. He wants me to let him down, I know.'

'Poor soul,' she said, looking at the woman struggling down the corridor.

'What was your mam like?'

'She was lovely,' said Midgley.

'She must have had him taped. She looks a grand woman. He's showed me photographs.' She took out her compact and made up her face. 'I'll go back and have another look. Then I've got to get over to a Round Table in Harrogate. Killed two birds with one stone for me, this trip.'

'Your mother'd not been dead a year,' sniffed Aunty Kitty. 'I was shocked.'

'I'm not shocked.'

'You're a man.'

'It wasn't like your dad. She's a cheek showing her face.'

'I'm rather pleased,' said Midgley.

'That hair's dyed,' said Aunty Kitty, but it was a last despairing throw. 'They're sending him downstairs tomorrow. He must be on the mend.' The drama was about to go out of her life. 'I only hope when he does come round he's not a vegetable.'

'I've told Shirley to ring if anything happens,' Valery said. 'Not that it will. His chest is better. His heart is better. He's simply unconscious now.'

Midgley was brushing his teeth.

'I'm looking forward to him coming round.' She raised her voice above the running tap. 'I long to know what his voice is like.'

'What?' said Midgley turning off the tap.

'I long to know what his voice is like.'

'Oh,' said Midgley. 'Yes.' And turned the tap on again.

'I think I know what it's like,' she said. 'I'd just like to have it confirmed.

'You don't seem to like talking about your father,' she said as she unzipped her skirt. 'Nice shirt.'

'Yes,' said Midgley. 'It's one of Dad's.'

'I like it.'

He went and had a pee and while he was out she took the receiver off the phone and put a cushion over it. When he came back she was already in bed.

'Hello,' he said, getting in and lying beside her. 'It's a bit daft is this.'

'Why?' she said. 'It happens all the time.'

'Yes,' said Midgley. 'So I'm told.'

They kissed.

'I ought to have done more of this.'

'What?'

'This,' said Midgley. 'This is going to be the rule from now on. I've got a lot of catching up to do.'

He ran his hand between her thighs.

'It's the nick of time.'

'First time I've heard it called that.'

'I hope this isn't one of those private beds,' said Midgley. 'I'm opposed to that on principle.'

'You've never asked me if I was married,' she said.

'You're a nurse. That puts you in a different category.' There was a pause. 'Are you married?'

'He's on an oil rig.'

'I hope so,' said Midgley.

Later on he had a cigarette and she had a cake.

'I was certain they were going to ring from the ward,' he said.

'No.' She lifted up the cushion and put the receiver back.

He frowned. Then grinned. 'No harm done,' he said.

They were just settling in again when the phone rang. She answered.

'Yes,' she said, looking at him. 'Yes.'

'What's the matter?' said Midgley.

She put the phone down and looked away.

He was already out of bed and pulling his trousers on.

'Had she rung before?'

She had turned to face the wall.

'Had she?' Midgley was shouting. 'Was she ringing?'

'Don't shout. There are night nurses asleep.'

At the end of the long corridor the doors burst open.

'It's the biggest wonder I'd not gone into see Mrs Tunnicliffe,' said Aunty Kitty. 'She's in Ward 7 with her hip. She's been waiting two years. But I don't know what it was. Something made me come back upstairs. I was sat looking at a *Woman's Own* then in walks Joyce and next minute the nurse is calling us in and he has his eyes open! So we were both there, weren't we.'

Mrs Midgley nodded. They were all three stood by the bedside.

'He just said, "Is our Denis here? Is our Denis here?"' said Aunty Kitty, 'and I said: "He's just coming, Frank." And he smiled a little smile and it was all over. Bless him. I was his only sister.'

The body lay flat on the bed, the eyes closed, the sheet up to the neck.

'The dot does something different when you're dying,' said Aunty Kitty, looking at the screen which now showed a continuous line. 'I wasn't watching it, naturally, but I noticed out of the corner of my eye it was doing something different during the last moments.'

'I think he's smiling,' said Mrs Midgley.

'Of course he's smiling,' said Midgley. He went and looked out of the window. 'He's won. Scored. In the last minute of extra time.'

Mrs Midgley came over to the window and said in an undertone: 'You disgust me.'

A nurse came in and switched off the monitor.

They went out.

'It's a pity you weren't here, Denis,' said Aunty Kitty. 'I mean when it came to the crunch. You've been so good. You've been here all the time he was dying. What were you doing?'

'Living,' said Midgley.

'He's at peace anyway,' said Aunty Kitty.

They went out and got his clothes. As they were walking

out a young man was on the phone. 'It's a boy!' he was saying. 'A boy! Yes. Just think. I'm a father.'

They stood in the car park.

'I suppose while we're here,' said Joyce, 'we could go up
home and make a start on going through his things.'

Withdrawn

For Every
Individual...

Renew by Phone
269-5222

Renew on the Web
www.indypl.org

For General Library Information
please call 275-4100

"A lively, charming coming-of-age story complete with farm-tested recipes."
—Publishers Weekly

"[Rochelle] Bilow brings sensuality to every scene, with rich descriptions of food and farm life, from washing freshly laid eggs to rendering lard. [She] offers readers a slow-cooked story, with tenderness and intermingled flavors enriched over time."
—Kirkus Reviews

"Rochelle Bilow brings tantalizing insight into the behind-the-scenes operations of a CSA farm, but also into the intricacies of falling in love. Until Bilow's book, I'd forgotten what a fragile dance it can be."
—CATHERINE FRIEND, author of *Hit by a Farm*,
The Compassionate Carnivore, and *Sheepish*

"A delicious memoir for anyone who has ever been drunk on the idea of farm love. You cannot help but cheer this farm girl on as she sings a bluesy ode to farm life and a complete love song to the table. The Blistered Tomato Gratin was amazing and the Bacon Maple Cornbread is going to be a regular around here for a long time. This girl can cook *and* write. It is a heady combination."
—ELLEN STIMSON, author of *Mud Season* and
Good Grief! Life in a Tiny Vermont Town

"Rochelle Bilow has done the impossible: make me want to live on a farm. I am not a farmer or a foodie or a female, and I couldn't put this down. She somehow makes churning butter sexy."
—JEFF WILSER, author of *The Maxims of Manhood*

THE EXPERIMENT
BECAUSE EVERY BOOK IS A TEST OF NEW IDEAS

"If you're looking for a book intimately detailing the circle of life for all inhabitants on a farm, including animals, vegetables, and humans, Rochelle Bilow's *The Call of the Farm* is the very thing. Covering a full year of living, working, cooking, and loving on a central NY farm, her book is candid, visceral, sincere, and delicious. I haven't been able to look at farmers' markets in the same way since reading it, and that's a very good thing."

—ASHLEY ENGLISH, author of *Handmade Living, A Year of Pies, Building Country Comforts*, and the Homemade Living series

"As gripping as a novel, *The Call of the Farm* immerses you in an aspiring food writer's journey from city to country as Rochelle Bilow falls in love with a farmer and learns to cook with real food. This beautifully written, honest, and vivid memoir sucks the reader in and lets us share Rochelle's failed attempts at butter churning, cold days of rock picking in the spring mud, and moments of delight finding companionship with a crew of like-minded farmers."

—ANNA HESS, author of *The Weekend Homesteader*

"If you've ever had romantic notions of farm life, Rochelle Bilow plays them out season by season in this sweet tell-all. Her experience brings readers into a world they'll likely never encounter first-hand, complete with honest-to-goodness farm-to-table living. The charming romance between her and a farmer (as well as the lifestyle itself) only heightens the storyline—and your appreciation for Bilow's all-in emotional journey."

—ERIN BYERS MURRAY, author of *Shucked: Life on a New England Oyster Farm*

"A delightful account of discovering the secret to health and happiness that so many people long for. Rochelle Bilow's memoir is a celebration of real food, the value of hard work and, of course, unbridled love. If you're intrigued by the simple, rural life, this book is for you!"

—TIM YOUNG, author of *The Accidental Farmers*

"A wonderfully entertaining story, pulling the reader ever deeper into Rochelle Bilow's year of farming and romance. Humorous, honest, and poignant, it is a compelling look into her life of cooking, loving, and living on a CSA farm."   —LEIGH TATE, author of *5 Acres & A Dream*